# FRUITS of MY SOLITUDE
## by
## Stephenie Monear-Schindler

Fruits of My Solitude, Copyrighted June 9, 2009 by Stephenie Monear-Schindler with the Library of Congress.
101 Independence Avenue SE, Washington, DC 20559-60000

All rights reserved. No part of this book may be reproduced, scanned, or distributed in any printed or electronic form without permission. Please do not participate in or encourage piracy of copyrighted materials in violation of the author's rights. Purchase only authorized editions.

Paperback ISBN-978-1-480286-184

Book cover design by Stephenie Monear-Schindler

**In Memory of
Kent January, Marc Dominguez,
& Leon Boyking**

# Preface

This book is an intimate view of the evolution of a mind and spirit that have been immersed in solitude; or an autobiography of a solitude, namely mine because of what was learned there. In the parallel story of my life where the source of my solitude is revealed there will be obvious holes in which information not pertinent to the purpose of my story is withheld. I thought very carefully about including those details, but that idea instantly soured in my mind knowing that some truths can burn up acres of valuable life if wielded by an unworthy motive. Too much negative information would clutter rather than assist in the telling of this story. Some knowledge of the harsh events of my youth are necessary to better understand how the solitude began, but are not intended to eclipse the focal point; the fruits; the hard won harvest which ripened in that solitary environment, which it is to be hoped the reader will come away with.

Everyone's story has a villain or two in it. Everyone has demons that they wrestle with…maybe mine showed up a little earlier than many people's. I'm sure it was this early induction into solitude that brought me to the realization of the enormity of life, what it can bring to any one of us, and how easy it is to fail that defused any desire I might once have felt to lynch the villains of my past. I believe that they, like I, will one day answer for their choices and deeds. At least from my vantage point in solitude, I've seen that everyone is eventually called into accountability in one way or another, no matter what his background or beliefs may be. So then, the objective of this story is to unveil an incredible solitude and the fruits it has produced in my life. My hope is that for anyone enduring an unwelcome solitude of their own, there might be found some help and peace in the pages ahead in seeing how much more productive and tolerable solitude can be when you pause to consider its positive side rather than looking at the world through its gates like a prisoner who will never be released. Prolonged solitude is like solitary confinement without the bars and concrete walls which in many ways is harder since you are always seeing possibilities that you could be a part of if only.... The prescription for successfully navigating an unwelcome solitude is to learn how to do the time without letting the time do you. Becoming embittered only deepens the solitude and ultimately cuts one off from future potential involvement in healthy relationships.

The deed to the land of solitude was mine at birth, handed to me at a very tender age long before I would finally learn how to keep my balance in its harsh terrain. I don't remember a specific beginning to it, only that as early as four years old, loneliness was familiar to me; not that I could have articulated it in that grown-up vernacular, but in the sense that I needed something outside of myself to be part of which I did not find. My lack of connection was a source of great anxiety. My lack of any endearing feelings for my adoptive parents confused me and caused much guilt and fear. I felt anchored to nothing. At four I felt alone.

The word solitude doesn't exist for young children nor are the reasons for its existence able to be pondered and rationalized by the mind of a four year old. All I knew was that it felt wrong, but it was all I knew and so it became my normal. At four you do perceive eyes that don't let you in, voices that push you away, body language that excludes you. At four you are deeply aware of someone's contempt for you. You just don't know the name of the emotion or the reason for its existence.

Eventually I would acquire a strong resolve not to push in where I knew I was not welcome, but my early need to belong was so urgent that it caused me to knock on many doors that I sensed were closed to me which over time tended to develop in me a poor self-image and shyness which I continue to battle with. However, I was by nature an optimist and every day I found something beautiful or interesting to increase and enliven my desert of solitude until it became a verdant and habitable paradise; a place I would seek, not run from; a place almost as much to be desired as companionship.

So why after coping with it all these years, do I need to talk about it now? Maybe it's because of the old Beatles song "Eleanor Rigby," that continues to haunt me after the years reminding me to look at "All the lonely people" and not only to ask "Where do they all come from? Where do they all belong?", but why must they be lonely at all? And how can I help? So much of the cause of unwelcomed solitude is simply a social lack of awareness. We don't really see people. And most of us are still in the position of Cain disputing with God about being our brothers' keeper. Too often we don't even feel adequate responsibility for the emotional well-being of those we know intimately and claim to love let alone acquaintances or perfect strangers.

But I believe we are responsible. Obviously not to the same extent with every person, but I contend that whoever we come into contact with, for whatever time we are in their presence, we have it within our power to smile, say a friendly word, have a temporary rant together about the dismal political scene, or whatever; to include, to make a positive connection with, whether for a few minutes in line at the bank, or for a lifetime as husband, wife, or friend. This seems to me a reasonable, basic human to human responsibility. The alternative is we can ignore, invalidate, or snub the people we encounter with any number of unkind responses reserved for those to whom we want to make it abundantly clear that they are neither entitled to nor worthy of even as tiny a morsel of civility as a smile from us.

I don't think most people understand the power they wield to do good or evil in the enormous arena of human contact. For instance, anyone who has ever gotten up on the wrong side of the bed (and that's everybody) knows how much even a simple kindness strategically placed can make the difference in the attitude you face the rest of the day with. Everything's gone wrong, you're late to your next appointment and the road you're driving on looks like a parking lot when all of a sudden someone beams a great smile, and signals you into a line of cars that is still moving at a snail's pace, but somehow it does lighten the present anxiety. For a few seconds you're connected. You catch yourself smiling a little and you let some other tired, cranky person in the 5mph parade and the phenomenon repeats itself.

There have been moments in my own life when I was so sad, that a smile from a stranger was crucial. And even though I needed much more than a smile, the unsolicited smile of kindness gave me strength, lightened my sadness, and allowed me to continue to hope. Whenever I hear on the news of tragedies such as the Columbine High School massacre or the Virginia Tech murders I feel not only the personal tragedy of the families of those who died at the hands of the gunmen, but also the tragedies of the gunmen who did not survive being consistently shut out by those around them. Instead of finding adequate fellowship, they were dehumanized and accordingly became inhuman. Our society unwittingly breeds many of these lamentable tragedies and then is chagrinned at the results.

My solitude began as a biracial child in the 1950's, adopted by an interracial couple whose marriage brought them the inevitable troubles that were so characteristic of but not exclusive to those years prior to the Civil Rights Movement, and if you were a mixed child of that era, you were going to get a belly full of being an outsider. Solitude is not generally appealing to young children, and I was not the exception to the rule.

Enforced isolation is nothing less than the boycotting of a human spirit, and believe me, if you are different in any way to some extent you will be isolated. I suppose it is society's dubious way of keeping unknown and potentially dangerous entities in check. It just doesn't seem to be a part of human make-up to jump to the alternate conclusion; that something different can be good. Certainly, there is much fear involved when society issues an edict against one group of humans having any associations with another group of humans, and God have mercy on the offspring of those forbidden unions. They are not usually welcome in either camp.

These social edicts remind me of a line spoken by the character Tevia from Fiddler on the Roof. In a close-knit Jewish community in Russia, in the early 1900's, Tevia (the father), is confronted by his daughter's taboo desire to wed a gentile with whom she has fallen in love. Besides his resolve to adhere to the laws of their faith, a good deal of his consideration was for the child they would have when he responded "A bird may love a fish, but where will they build their home?" The question had merit, especially considering the times they lived in. Certainly as the century progressed in our own country with the social line of division between whites and blacks clearly delineated, many parents of young people considering interracial marriage found themselves confronted with the same deep concerns for their grandchildren who would be born of those unions and would bear enormous repercussions at the hands of a disapproving society. It was not an unreasonable concern in either setting.

My first sixteen years of life as a mixed child in an all-black neighborhood set the stage for a solitude that would continue for most of my life. By the time I got to junior high, my life of segregation was over and the unavoidable head-on collision with white folks brought a whole new element of resistance to my life; still not accepted, but for a variety of different reasons. On the one hand I dealt with the unwarranted jealousy/resentment of a sizable portion of the black community, and on the other hand, the incongruous mix of curiosity and reproachful, stigmatic opinion I too frequently encountered in the white world.

When you are pushed away consistently, sometimes even brutally, and even by those who profess to care; when there is no world you can fit into, eventually you begin to believe that the problem really does lie with you as though there were a visible stamp on you that warns others away. But for an optimist like me, negativity was something to be fought off because it was not beautiful, and I wanted what was beautiful, and I desperately wanted truth. It was at that time that I made the perhaps unconscious decision to embellish my solitude with as many beautiful and meaningful pursuits as I could. Things unfolded around me, unaware of me.  It was a fly-on-the-wall experience, almost embryonic at times.

My first recollection that I was not welcome among other children, and that even some adults seemed to have strong objections to my presence was when I was four years old, but even though it was bewildering to me because I did not at all understand the why of it, somewhere inside there was an intuitive notion that the hate displayed by the children was a learned and reflected hate. I cannot now, nor could I believe then that such young minds and hearts understand the ramifications of their hatred any more than they really understand the salvation of love, though obviously, I could not have framed those intuitions with the words I now write.

All these things I felt in my heart, but being a child, my analytical thought processes were quite fuzzy.  I would not recognize for many years yet to come that not only was there prejudice between whites and blacks, but also, the often unacknowledged prejudice within the black race towards those who were either too light-skinned, or too dark to fit into the mainstream. There finally came a time people no longer threw stones or spewed out the poison in their minds, and public rejection lessened, or at least was more covert, partly due to real maturity in some, and in others simply because there was a social understanding that it was no longer politically correct or in style to hate for those particular reasons any more.  But in my case, even though the forces that formed my solitude had somewhat abated, the habit of it became a continuing reality.

Also, as an adult I noticed that because my life was seven eights solitude that whenever I did make a meaningful connection, it was instantly in danger of being overwhelmed by the outpouring of that solitude.  I have frequently joined myself to people who were either slightly or extremely enamored with the otherworldliness that emanates from those who dwell in solitude. At first they are attracted to the mystery that surrounds the solitary person.  But often after they connect with that solitary one and the mystery morphs into a revelation of the real person, it destroys the fantasy.

But the one in solitude does not want to remain a mystery, but wants to know and be known and to share all the beauty that was accumulated in solitude.

Solitude is an enormous world of opportunity regardless of its origins. For the brave it becomes the frontier of one's own self-discovery; a place to find out who we really are, and to discover the strengths and weaknesses in our characters; to preserve and protect the worthwhile parts of us, and to work on the parts that displease us; to get an unclouded view of our true intentions regarding every single facet of life. In solitude you weigh your pain, assess the damage, and give yourself a hopeful prognosis. In solitude, you become your own mother. In growing awareness, which is the by-product of a fruitful solitude, you become the guardian of your own soul.

Solitude is certain to be experienced by all at some point in life. There is even the preferred solitude of some people for whom it is just easier not to have to attend to any other human being or situation than themselves, and to avoid like death becoming involved in anything that would require reciprocation on their part.

Nothing particular is required of us in solitude, nor must we be physically alone to experience it, for whenever there is no true connection, there will always be solitude. So many rooms; so much space in solitude. Some rooms are frightening and we tiptoe past those doors hoping not to disturb the demons inside. We hope that voice will not start, because once it does, no other voice of reason will be loud enough to banish the fear and doubt it instills in us. Some rooms we go in just to relax, and then there are rooms which have much promise if only we would spend some time there to sort through the confusion and misconceptions, and update our thoughts concerning issues we made hard and fast decisions about long before we were qualified to have opinions on them. There are treasures we take out in the privacy of our being to bestow unadulterated feelings on, feelings we don't want anyone else to know about, and of course those shames and failures for which we stand trial over and over again. In that sequestered place, we can go ahead and ask ourselves the deep questions whose answers we would be disinclined to reveal in their entirety anywhere else.

Sadly, when solitude has been an intimate part of your reality, you almost need someone to come in and rescue you from it; invite you into their world and prove that you are welcome there. Not being accepted can be a bitter solitude unless you get the determination to not allow your detractors to imprison you, but instead make that solitude a large and profitable experience.

Solitude is a place of possibilities, where damaged hope can be repaired, shined up, and reassigned to life. Peace is not always a given even if the circumstances of life seem lined up in your favor. Sometimes it must be fought for in the confines of solitude.

SCM-S

# Contents

| | | |
|---|---|---|
| Prologue | My Earthly Eden-Acres in the Mind | 13 |
| Chapter 1- | The Beginning of Solitude | 18 |
| Chapter 1 | Part 2-A Detour | 52 |
| Chapter 2- | The Village That Raised the Child | 79 |
| Chapter 3- | True Short Stories | 126 |
| Chapter 4- | The Perilous Solitude | 153 |
| Chapter 5- | Observations in Solitude | 164 |
| Chapter 6- | Occupying Solitude-The Fruits | 173 |
| Chapter 7- | Fruit for Thought | 184 |
| Chapter 8- | The Inspirational Solitude | 200 |
| Afterword | Who Are We | 209 |

# ..Prologue

## My Earthly Eden - Acres in the Mind

Medicine acres; perhaps the most poignant, hauntingly beautiful place in my life, and certainly my most frequently visited memories are those of Medicine Acres. Photos give evidence that I was at Medicine Acres as early as a year old. My personal memories do not go back so far, but begin at about age three. Without a doubt, this extraordinary place fostered in me a permanent affinity with beauty, and an acute sense of wonder in the great outdoors that not only hasn't diminished but has deepened over time providing thousands of hours of bliss. It was also there that I first entered into an awareness of my solitude.

Medicine Acres was an abundant and sizable piece of land located in Holly, Michigan. I never did know what the acreage was, but it contained a lake whose shores my eyes could not find; a row of small white cabins that were only two skipping heartbeats from the lake, and nearby streams that sparkled and shimmered like diamonds under the brilliant summer sun. There were hills and meadows that were warmly alive and cool emerald woods where golden pools of sunshine spilled between the branches onto the grass-bare paths beneath. Uninterrupted skies were continually transforming from beauty to beauty with such vivid and tender colors that it never failed to produce a quiet, but deep thrill in me just to look at them. Whenever I was there, I felt so close to the sun, water, wind and especially the woods and sky, that in a strange way I came to think of them as mine; they were my first real friends and as aware of me as I was of them.

This little Eden I was told, belonged to two women doctors whom I much later found out were lesbians. Just what my adoptive parents' relationship to them was or even how they met, I never knew, for the only mention I'd ever heard of them was in connection to their lake property. That said, my memories of them are quite vague bordering on nonexistent, for though we spent a lot of time at Medicine Acres, I only ever recall seeing them from the car a couple of times when for some reason or other, my parents had to drive up the hill to their home. My world however, because of my adoptive parents interracial marriage, was well populated with the misfits of society with whom they were friends, and so I met many people who were for a variety of reasons exiled from the main stream. These ladies, obviously fell into their ranks. It never occurred to me to judge these societal outcasts. All those rejected by society must form their own society. While this may seem to have been an unremitting tragedy in the minds of the so called normal, the consequences provided some rare experiences especially for one as young as myself. People who are locked out find some ingenious ways to make it work for them. Being ostracized requires some imagination to survive.

Accordingly, my adoptive parents being outcasts because of their marriage, had no condemnation toward others in the same fix for different reasons, and held the view that as long as it did not concern or affect them personally, what other people did was their own affair and no one else's and so these lady doctors likewise fell under no particular scrutiny. That they really liked my adoptive parents, and had invited them and any friends they might choose to bring to spend as much time at the lake as they wanted was not in the least strange to me.

The only other person I remember seeing there was a black man named Joe whose deep-lined ebony face was so dark you could scarcely make out his features in broad day light. His job was care-taker of the grounds of Medicine Acres. I once saw him kill a rattle-snake which he held up on a stick for me to examine. He said they made a fine stew which sounded nasty to me. "Tastes like chicken." He said. But I had a deep conviction that I'd never find out.

Every year as soon as fine weather set in, my mother would pack up food, suntan lotion, towels, good books, swimsuits, me, and the family's Boston Terrier, Dandy, and we would be off to Medicine Acres for as much time as could be stolen. Sometimes we were there for weeks, sometimes days and sometimes only the remaining hours after the work day ended. But whenever we went, next to visiting my grandmother, it was the most exciting event in my life. Usually, it was my mother and me who went early in the morning, and were joined by my father who came as soon as he could after work. They loved the water and both were excellent swimmers. In fact, it was at Medicine Acres that I first learned of some of the resourceful plotting involved in their early courtship. Other than these little snippets of their past, I knew precious little of what their lives were like before I came on the scene.

Since both my adoptive parents were excellent swimmers and had lived across a lake from each other, they used to each swim to the middle of the lake and there they would talk and flirt, and plan the future while treading water. Also, my father had a gift for whistling beautifully; not the squeaky five-note range of most people, but a whistle clear and sweet with all the flexibility of an instrument. He would sometimes pass by my mother's home whistling a tune which would signal to her his destination, so that she would know where to meet him.

Sometimes, when I think of those young lovers, their expectations, hope and zeal, extinguished by the hatefulness of this world, I grieve. By the time I had come into their lives they were foundering in the final stages of the death of those expectations.

I believe Medicine Acres was as much a refuge for my adoptive parents as it was for the women who bought it. Perhaps the respite it offered kept their relationship from completely disintegrating, I certainly felt much less tension between them in this setting than in any other and it was definitely a safe haven for me. As soon as we pulled into the long, hilly, sun-drenched path that led to the cabins and the lake, I would begin to laugh and to bounce up and down in the back seat of the car with excitement. Our Boston Terrier, Dandy, who thought all car-rides ended at the dreaded veterinarian's office didn't appreciate my enthusiasm and usually growled a warning for me to keep well to my own side of the back seat.

My mother would pull the car directly in front of the cabins on the tire-worn turf and turned me and Dandy loose while she unloaded the car. I didn't like the cabins very well. They were small and dark, and damp smelling. There was a row of about six cabins all sparsely decked out with two beds apiece, a toilet, sink, and crude shower, a small refrigerator and a two-burner stove; all the provision anybody needs at a beautiful lake. Swim, sun, eat, sleep, dream, walk, read, and explore, then start over.

Once the car was unloaded, we would head down the gently sloping hill just in front of the cabins. There lay a sun twinkling lake with one dock and an enormous boulder about a dozen steps from its shoreline. I always ran straight down to the water ahead of my mother. In the shallows it was mirror clear and I smiled at my reflection in the water where minnows swam, silver sides flashing in the sunlight. The smell of the lake was a powerful part of its charm for me. To this day, the smell of a lake in one sniff can plug me in to a thousand compelling memories, and longings to return once more to Medicine Acres.

Swim suited, ice tea in hand, my mother would sit on the dock with her feet dangling in the water sometimes throwing a ball or sticks for the dog to swim after while I sat like a princess on *my* boulder watching the sky, with the beautiful blue Dragonflies darting here and there. After letting the effects of Medicine Acres settle into us, my mother would have a cigarette and then a swim, Dandy would get under a tree for a nap, and I would be off exploring; a dusty, barefoot gypsy child in my own personal heaven. Medicine Acres was a living fairytale of which I got to be a part; one of two places on earth I felt completely at home in.

By the time I was ten or so, we no longer went to Medicine Acres. I never knew why. Maybe the Doctors sold the land, or died. But I have never ceased to think of it as one of the most important experiences of my life leaving a wonderfully indelible memory. I often long for Medicine Acres, and never more than a couple days go by that it is not fondly and warmly remembered for some adventure or other. Even now, I'm believing God is partial to that morsel of land.

# Chapter 1

# The Beginning of Solitude

# The Sky Opens

"Then said I, "Ah Lord God, Behold I cannot speak: for I am a child."
Jeremiah 1:6

To give a careful and honest account of my solitude and in what soil its seeds were sown, a glimpse into the lives of my adoptive parents is necessary; the times they lived in, and the circumstances preceding my birth are integral parts of my own story. And so, I begin before my beginning.

My adoptive parents' marriage was a classic example of many unions which were once passionate but whose original connection was somehow eroded by the pressures of this life leaving them to cope in the void. Obviously, they must have been very connected at some point to have bypassed all convention to be together, but whatever it was that brought them together was either long gone or too severely damaged to nourish either of them by the time I arrived.

They lived completely separate lives, coming together briefly over coffee each morning to set the days' affairs in order. Even as a small child I remember feeling disturbed at the detachment I saw and felt between them. My father was a man so deeply absorbed with his ongoing work with the UAW that he was usually emotionally inaccessible and left all aspects of home life to my mother. Many years later his very obituary was a testament of his away-from-home commitments and activities. It took a full two columns in the newspaper to list the myriad organizations he belonged to and committees he actively served on. My mother had no part in his daily life outside the home and was on her own when it came to filling the empty spaces of her life. She was much more limited in her choices of recreation than most women of her acquaintance since her interracial marriage separated her widely from her peers.

All through time mixed marriages between most races have generally been viewed with a better-let-that-alone attitude, but between blacks and whites they were extraordinarily taboo before the Civil Rights era; about as welcome as the plague and dealt with in much the same way: Isolation. There were no afternoons of shopping with friends, or special occasions with relatives, for except for her mother, the rest of her family felt justified in having nothing to do with her. Added to her isolation, my adoptive mother was childless and the hope of children was finally extinguished after several miscarriages that eventually led to a hysterectomy. Then in her mid-forties with an empty marriage, no close friends, no children, and no road back to the past, the future must have appeared rather bleak.

It was during this period of time that a single event was to forever change her life. Because my adoptive parents were unable to take part even in such simple social activities as eating out, they entertained at home. The people who made up this social circle were, like my adoptive parents, not welcome elsewhere because of their interracial relationships, or whatever traditionally objectionable lifestyle they happened to be a part of. Now, for the time being, they all had a place to hang out and to enjoy some semblance of normalcy in the company of others with similar troubles; a retreat from the racially charged social dramas that were an inescapable part of the lives they'd chosen.

Among the couples who had found a week-end refuge in the home of Earl and Eleanor C. were my biological parents, John J. and Shirley S. He was a middle-aged, married black man and she was a young, unmarried, white girl. My future adoptive parents knew John, but had never known Shirley. John had been invited to the house parties with the understanding that he needn't come alone. He took them up on the invitation, but it must be noted that upon meeting, Shirley and Eleanor had an almost instant dislike of one another which over time developed into an active contempt. Understanding the angst between these two women is of pivotal importance to this story.

Because nature works, it wasn't long before Shirley was in trouble; pregnant and apparently without any resources to weather a storm of the magnitude she was in for. She'd lose her job and receive very little if any sympathy, and plenty of condemnation. What relatives she had would neither approve nor support her.

To jump ahead just a little, the story I was told by my adoptive mother almost as soon as I could speak (without the perspective of my biological mothers' input), I believe was calculated to distance me from everyone except her, not out of viciousness, but out of her own need. She mentioned on more than one occasion that my biological father, John J. was neither responsible nor decent; that the *help* he had offered was to sell me to a couple up north for six hundred dollars. This information about my real father instantly cauterized any desire I might have ever had to meet him which I later suspected was the intention of the revelator. I grew up only a mile or so from where he lived, but I'd been forewarned that he didn't want to see me or have anything to do with me. Many years later when he died, one of the many brothers I'd met brought his obituary to me. I read it minus any feeling of loss whatever. Inside I felt the world was better off without him since he had completely walked away from the children he'd brought into the world without a backward glance. Though I was seemingly unmoved by his death, there was still a disturbing lack of closure to the end of this father I'd never even met.

To return to the natural order of these events, once Shirley's pregnancy became evident, there was a glimmer of hope for Eleanor in the regrettable circumstances. She knew a child of mixed racial heritage would be an enormous disadvantage for a young, unmarried, white woman, and she also knew that it was as good an opportunity as she would ever have to be a parent since interracial couples were not eligible to adopt children. Attached to the information that Eleanor C. shared with me about my real parents, I was also told that Earl C. was not exactly in harmony with her on her parenting aspirations, but got reluctantly on board when he heard of my biological fathers' plan to sell me.

With this reluctant go-ahead, Eleanor wasted no time in approaching Shirley. The proposed arrangement was that Shirley would stay in their home until my birth. Food, clothing, and medical care would be provided all with the understanding that when I was born, I would be given over to Eleanor C. to be raised. Shirley was not ready to have children and didn't really want me, and so the arrangement was accepted...or at least this is the story that was told to me....

Decades later in a talk I had with Shirley, a very different story surfaced. When I first met her, the story did not all tumble out at once as one might suppose. In fact, she never willingly spoke of it for years. Bits and pieces came over time with my guarded interrogations. Shirley is a shy and reserved person, not completely easy in company or conversation and it was easy to see that she'd fought a lot of demons concerning her decisions regarding me; easy to see the scars that had been left because of them. But it had been her habit not to discuss the past. Discussing it with me didn't make it any easier but at last it seemed the time had come for her to tell her side of the story. As she told me what had happened, emotion caused her to pause often in telling a story that had been kept deep inside for so long that it was difficult to relive it. There was palpable pain both in the telling and the hearing.

*When Shirley found out that she was pregnant, she truly did not have any place to go and what little family she had, she did not want to ask for help. She said that because of her extreme dislike for Eleanor, that if she'd had any other choice, she would have taken it in a heartbeat. But when she told John, he did not shirk the responsibility as I had been told, but paid for most of what she needed during her stay with Eleanor C. He also, did not try to sell me to a couple up north, but was very much against my being kept by Earl and Eleanor. He'd known them for a number of years and was extremely reluctant to see a child of his reared in their home. Shirley also told me that John's wife with whom he had two sons was also quite willing to raise me, but that John was understandably uncomfortable with having his wife raise a child that he'd had no business fathering in the first place.*

I met his wife many years later who affirmed that she had wanted me since she'd had no daughter of her own. She confessed to me that over the years she had often driven to my neighborhood about a mile from her own house to get a look at me, saying how pretty she thought I was and how much I looked like John.

As Shirley's pregnancy came to an end and I was born, her depression deepened knowing that as soon as she recovered respecting her agreement with Eleanor, she would be expected to leave. She had wanted me; she just didn't have any way of supporting us and felt that at least with Eleanor I would have the things I needed. When I was three weeks old she left, but came back now and then to see me. She said the visits were extremely painful for her especially when it was time to leave me again, and that she cried for days afterward. Finally, she came to the conclusion that perhaps it would be better for her, better for me, if she didn't come to see me anymore, though she said that over the years Eleanor had called her on many occasions when my behavior had perplexed her. In the meantime, Shirley said she grieved and marked my birthdays and planted a tree in her front yard which she named for me. I have seen the tree. It's a good sized spruce. She also planted trees for each of my brothers.

For most of my life I've lived under the burden of what Eleanor C. had planted in my head as a very young child; that I had not been wanted by anyone but her. To that end she did her best to sever every emotional connection or hope I might have outside of her. I spent a good deal of my youth believing that my real parents were bad people and that as a direct result, I too, was bad; conceived at a party by a young, unmarried woman and a man cheating on his wife; a mistake, unwanted, a bad seed. I somehow felt I could never rise above that station and therefore was unworthy of love, or even a place of esteem in anyone's life.

When I finally understood the sad history, the almost comedic irony behind the scenes, I was at an emotional loss as to how to process the whole thing. How could I have known as a child the hearty animosity that existed between the woman who gave birth to me and the one who raised me? It was those beginning components of basic discord that were to be the first bricks in the wall that slowly built up between my adoptive mother and me over the years. I didn't understand the resistance I felt towards her, but it was there from my earliest memory, perhaps about three years old. I remember a simple but very specific dream I had when I was four.

*In the dream I was a giant child standing in the bathroom over our enormous claw foot bathtub, my head touching the high ceiling. My miniature adoptive mother was taking a bath. I leaned over, put my hand into the water and grabbed the chain on the rubber plug and pulled it out. The water and Eleanor started to go down the drain. She was screaming and begging me to save her, but I stood silently by, letting her go, glad to be rid of her.*

This dream was intensely troubling to me, and I felt very guilty for having dreamt it, but I now believe that dream to have been evidence of my suppressed feelings or lack thereof for my mother and my desire to escape her.

I also had no idea how very much like my birth-mother I was, and it was those genetic similarities that chafed at Eleanor. Even as a very young child I always felt that she didn't quite like me. She often remarked how she was almost glad whenever I was sick, because it was the only time I would allow her to hold or pet me. Looking back, I feel sad for Eleanor. Her expectations in me were sorely disappointed, and her need to be loved and needed complicated and unsatisfied. This also points to a huge consideration for those who intend to adopt; you should be aware that you are not getting a blank sheet of paper to write on. Since that child has a self that is partly genetic, you should be prepared to find unfamiliar characteristics in him/her.

I suppose my infancy passed without too much out of the ordinary happening. My earliest memories of childhood, which are surprisingly clear, begin in my third and fourth year. This was the first time I remember having any awareness that there was something wrong between my parents. Though I was obviously too young to analyze the sharp words, red swollen eyes, separate bedrooms, and the detachment of their entire relationship, it weighed on me in a vague and unsettling way. There was no way for me to understand at my tender age how much Eleanor C. had been depending on me to mend her broken life and bring some sort of happiness and meaning to it. Though she never spoke directly about it, I always felt a sort of pressure that something was expected of me.

Life went on, and the unnatural became the natural. We were not anything like what a real family should be like, though we settled into a norm for us, each one of us occupying ourselves with our several differing interests; Earl C. with his work, Eleanor with her ongoing projects and hobbies, plus raising me, and me in the world of solitude that I came to love and depend on.

In those quiet places there was respite from that nagging sense of wrongness. For me, from my early post toddler years it was a window-seat, from whose perch I watched the birds and squirrels, or hidden among the leaves in the neighbors grape arbor where I quietly enjoyed the rich aroma and sweet-tart taste of the grapes. There was also a very imposing, and to me quite exotic painting in an ancient frame that Eleanor hung in each home we lived in. It was usually placed in a seldom used room; an Italian villa in warm colors with several verandas and outdoor staircases that led to flowered, vine-covered landings. It also had a small boathouse, and all of this was set against a great body of water with a lonely looking mountain in the background. It appealed very much to my romantic imagination and I would stare at it for hours sometimes, seeing myself with friends playing in the boathouse or standing on the shore throwing rocks into the water. In later years as I stared at the picture, I received my first kiss from a boy who didn't even know I was alive on one of the flowered landings just below my imaginary bedroom. So many of my daydreams took place in that painting and ironically, it was the only thing that my adoptive parents left me in their will.

Another occupation of mine was to run away periodically. From the time I was four, I began to disappear to my parents' continual anxiety. The family dog, a Boston terrier named Dandy who'd previously been trained as a Seeing Eye dog, accompanied me on my rambles and took respectable care of me, but a couple of times the police were called. One particular occasion was when Dandy and I had dropped in on a slightly senile, elderly woman. All I knew was that she was extremely generous with her cookies and had a piano which she allowed me play without let or hindrance. But I can certainly appreciate the alarm a parent must feel at not knowing where their four year old is at10:00pm on a summer's night.

We had a fenced yard with a padlocked gate and thereafter I was locked in, but I was quite gifted at getting away. My immense curiosity and ambition to get beyond my own yard was all the incentive I needed to accomplish my escapes, and so I continued to go missing from time to time. My parents gave up trying to lock me in, and instead made me learn our phone number and address so that I could call them from wherever I landed in my rambles. It was a safer world then, and I was a regular sight wandering around with my dog, to neighbors, to the churches in the area, to the neighborhood police; to the drugstore proprietor a couple of blocks away where I transacted many an ice cream deal. I don't believe I was in much danger then. Later that year (still at four years old), I went to the hospital to have my tonsils removed and disappeared in the hospital prior to surgery. (See "A Medical Adventure" in Chapter. True Short Stories). I've always believed I was looking for a connection. I had sort of an odd habit of trying to look into the eyes of everyone I saw, always with the feeling of looking for something in them that I could not name. I still do.

There were lots of diversions to fill in the void I felt so pressingly, all wonderful each in their own way, but my favorite pastime of all which moved me more than all the other diversions put together was to watch the sky. Anytime I felt hurt or confused, the sky was my sole comforter. I felt like the sky was the only thing on my side. I know it sounds a bit crazy to an adult, but as a child I felt that the sky liked me and cared very much for me. Children don't know much about personifications, but they invent them whenever they feel the need.

Eleanor, on the other hand, was comforted by the endless stream of projects that she kept going. She loved reading and almost any kind of art that allowed her to exercise her creativity. One of her favorite hobbies was ceramics, and for hours on end she would form and paint the graceful figurines. After each process they had to be fired and since she didn't have a kiln of her own, she used a kiln belonging to a lady who had been in the same art class with her and who had generously offered her the use of it anytime she might need it.

One summer evening in 1955, Eleanor gathered up her latest figurines that needed firing, wrapped each one carefully and put them in a box. As I came in the house from playing in the backyard, she called to me to go to the bathroom, wash my face and hands and get ready to leave. The woman whose kiln she used lived out in the country, a considerable distance from us. Familiar with her hobby schedules, I knew on what errand we were headed. Shopping I hated, but a ride in the car at sunset on a summer's eve was something to look forward to.

Some of my happiest early memories are of car rides; trips to Jackson, Michigan to see my grandmother; drives to Medicine Acres to swim in the lake: drives up north with my mother and grandmother; and trips to the country. Tonight would be a pleasant evening for me, riding down dirt roads and watching the sky from the backseat of the car and singing to myself. The only negative to riding in the car with either parent was their incessant smoking. Nothing's perfect, but at least it was summer and the windows would be down.

Little did I suspect that this evening was going to separate itself from all others by bringing me into the crosshairs of the Eternal. I remember as though it were yesterday, that while I watched the sunset all pink and gold and deep purple, that the song I was singing got stuck in my throat and hurt because a lump was there, and there were tears pouring down my face, and powerful emotions I'd never felt before opening me...but to what?

I felt strange, confused, alarmed but not frightened, and at the same time I wanted to get as close to what I was feeling as possible. Being hurt or unhappy were my only experiences with tears, yet while the tears ran down my face I was neither hurt nor unhappy. I wanted the feeling to last. I felt close to something for the first time in my small life, but what was it? I did realize that my response was connected in some way to the sky. I'll never know how long that moment settled into my soul, but I clearly remember not wanting it to leave.  I had been waiting for something to happen and now it was happening. For the first time in my small life I felt something interrupting the isolation I was so used to.  It was as if company had come specifically to visit me. To say I was completely overwhelmed is a colossal understatement!

After a few minutes of this powerful new awareness of I-don't-know-what my ability to speak returned.  I broke in on my mother's reverie to ask "Who made the sky?" I had always been impressed with the beautiful things she made of clay, but the splendor of that sunset, and the feelings which accompanied it far surpassed anything she had ever done. I felt an urgent desire to meet the one who could make a sky like that. Absentmindedly my mother answered "God made it." I digested this in silence. Then other thoughts began to flood my mind. "Who made the trees, the grass, dogs, cats, the snow and rain?  Who made me?" By this time I was going on so that I don't think I was listening very much. Finally, in the impatient voice that one hears after asking too many questions came the final answer, "God made it all."

For the second time in my life, (and in the same hour yet) I was at a loss for words.  It's one thing to be quiet in solitude; it's quite another to be struck dumb by revelation.  My parents were not church-going folks, so as of yet I knew absolutely nothing of spiritual matters. What I did know, though I could not have put it into words at the time, was that something wonderful had happened to me, and I meant not to let it go, so I continued to watch the sky only now with great expectations.

## My First Road Map

The revelation of God and His spectacular creation spawned a million questions in my little head which I wasted no time in asking. I was told by everyone that I asked more questions than any ten children put together, and in retrospect, I almost feel sorry for my mother for my unremitting assault on her time and energy.

"Where does God live?" I wanted to know.

"In Heaven." was her reply. I became concerned when I heard that I probably wasn't going to be going anytime soon.

"How do people get to know God?" I asked.

When it was explained to me that most people went to church to find out about God, I knew instantly that I wanted to go to church and asked if we could go right now. I was disappointed to hear that I'd have to wait until Sunday. I had absolutely no notion that there were different kinds of churches, and as near as I could gather, my parents pretty much held the view that it didn't really matter where you went. My mother was pretty sure she was just as close to God while working in her garden as she would be at church. But apparently it did matter where you went, because as soon as I made my choice of churches known (actually it was the only church I knew of), I was scowled at and told "NO!" in no uncertain terms. You see, just across the street from our house, so close you could hit it with a stone, was Harris Temple, a sanctified church. This of course, had no particular meaning for me at the time, but the reason it seemed so appealing was that most church nights in summer they left their doors open, and I was spellbound with interest as I watched the strange and animated goings-on from my bedroom window when I was supposed to be asleep. There was singing, and shouting, pianos and trumpets, tambourines and dancing. There seemed to be a fever pitch of excitement from beginning to end. I wanted very much to go to that church, but my mother was adamantly against it. If I wanted to go to church all that bad, I could just go down the street to the Baptist church. Arguing with your parents was not an option when I was a child, so the following Sunday, washed and dressed in my best clothes, I set out to go to Sunday school at the Baptist church.

The Pastor and his wife were wonderfully caring people, and really my first examples of Godly living. Reverend and Mrs. Courts had no children of their own at the time and so poured out their love richly on all the children of that congregation. Mrs. Courts was not only our Sunday school teacher, but also the Kindergarten teacher at Stewart School where I would be attending in the fall. She was always particularly kind to me which drew me to her, and looking back I realize that she was very much aware of and truly cared about my outcast state and the constant harshness with which I was treated being the only mixed child in an all-black school. She always seemed to be around for me when trouble was brewing. One particular event stands out vividly in my mind.

During my second grade year, our school was having a play. It seemed like half the kids at school were in it. For my part, I had a very beautiful full length raspberry colored dress of satin that my mother had had made for the occasion. I was to wear it in the second act of the play. After our final dress rehearsal, everyone left their costumes in the dressing rooms since the play was to take place the following evening. Just before the curtain rose on our little play, Mrs. Courts took me back to the dressing room to help me get my dress on only to discover my beautiful dress was badly ripped in several places. I think she was even more upset than I was. With eyebrows knit furiously together over fiery eyes, pursed lips, and intermittent bursts of indignation under her breath, she rummaged around in her sewing kit and began to sew faster than I could have imagined humanly possible. When Act 2 rolled around I made my entrance on stage without spot or wrinkle. I'm sure someone was disappointed, but it wasn't me thanks to Mrs. Courts!

It was about the time I began going to the Courts' church that my awareness of being *different* reached another level. All attempts at becoming socially involved only seemed to highlight my offending difference. I just couldn't understand the hate directed at me. It bewildered me continually. Often I would go outside in search of someone to play with only to be chased away by angry faces and voices. The children closer to my own age were not yet tainted by prejudice and jealousy, but some of the older kids educated them by example how I was to be thought of and treated. Many times I arrived home with crayons broken to pieces; coloring books ripped to shreds and decapitated dolls. Sometimes I came home at track record speeds dodging stones thrown and names called. I didn't know what the shouted epithets half-breed and high-yella meant, or the whispered word mulatto from disapproving grown-ups, but I knew that they were not good things. In my elementary school years the prevailing wind of my emotions was fear, but the time was not far off when a consuming anger would eclipse that fear. Many of the grown-ups were as unmerciful as the children, and while it was unexpected, it somehow did not surprise me. Somewhere inside me I instinctively felt that the children's attitudes toward me were direct descendants of their parents' hatreds.

Though the matter was far from clear to me then, there was one incident in particular that brought home to me how objectionable an association I was considered to be by others, and I became a first-hand witness to how an adult can transfer negative judgments to their children and with what speed those transfers are absorbed.

The incident occurred when I was about seven or eight years old; I remember that it was on a perfect, mid-summer afternoon with a stainless blue sky that I was playing in the front yard of a little girl named Darla who lived around the corner from me. About an hour or so into our playtime another girl was dropped off by her parents to spend the night. The little girl who was dropped off was someone I'd always wanted to be friends with and when I found out she was to spend the night, I was filled with excitement and hoped that I would be invited to stay too, but when Darla, (who at this point was as anxious to have me stay as I was), ran over to ask her mother if I could stay the night, I could feel in an instant that her mother neither liked me nor wanted me to be an all-night guest. If I'd been just a little older, my pride would've prevented me from staying anywhere I was not welcome, but I was very young and I wanted desperately to belong…enough to push my way in and try to ignore the rejection I felt. Darla's mother was somewhat put on the spot with me standing there with hopeful eyes like a lost puppy looking for a home, and with scarcely concealed resentment, she said I could stay. I remember too, my mother's strange reluctant consent to my being allowed to stay in their home. She knew exactly what kind of treatment I was about to experience, but felt powerless to protect me from the hurts that were surely coming my way. Young as I was, I would have to learn about people for myself. Eventually, I would be able to spot prejudice anywhere, anytime, and in anyone, no matter how many teeth were showing in a grin. Then I would be cagey and solitary, but for now I was very young, and every day was a brand new day full of possibilities. And this day I was going to spend the night with others and belong!

No amount of wishful thinking was going to change Darla's mothers' mind about me. All through the evening she hung over me like a dark rain cloud, scowling at me and beaming a great smile at them---I felt these exaggerated contrasts were especially for my benefit. She expressed her disapproval in many covert ways. I was seated away from the others during supper, and later I could hear the girls whispering and giggling through the night from the bedroom I had been placed in down the hall. As the night wore on the girls caught on to her example that I was to be excluded and then they began to mimic her snobbery. They would have followed her lead for good or for evil. She chose to be an evil example and accordingly, they followed suit. This incident was a kind of turning point for me, though of course I was hardly aware of the changes that were subtly taking place in my thinking and in my responses to the inside racial idiocy I was continually subjected to.

These sorts of experiences were the standard fare of my childhood. I was even forbidden to enter the homes of my adoptive mother's relatives. But to my grandmother who loved me, this was an outrage not to be tolerated, and she wasted no time in taking a stand against all of them on my behalf. To this day, it's still amazing to me how the love of one can counteract the hatred of many. My grandmother, Esther Jones, became the mainstay of my young life, but more and more as the harshness of my situation dawned on me, my thoughts turned inward and to God.

Returning to the chronological order of my story, one Sunday morning at church near the end of my fourth summer, Reverend Courts announced a contest that would be taking place among the older Sunday school children. Anyone able to recite the books of the Bible would win the prize of a brand new Bible. He held it up for everyone to see. It was white with bright gold letters on it, and I felt I just had to have it. I hadn't paid attention to the fact that the contest was for the older children, so I ran straight home to ask my mother about the Bible. I was told that it was the Word of God; the way God spoke to people. Maybe He would talk to me!! The fact that I was only four and could not read yet had absolutely no bearing whatsoever on my desire to have the Bible for my own, so I began to pester my mother to teach me its' books. She was always reading something and belonged to several book clubs. She read to me often and was always talking about the advantages of reading, a good vocabulary, and the adventure of going many places in a book that we might not otherwise have opportunities to visit, so, I felt confident that she would approve my request. After all, there was not only knowledge to dispense, but surely some humorous entertainment in hearing a four year old say "Habakkuk, Ezekiel, or Zephaniah." Under her tutelage I was soon able to say them easily and looked forward to the contest. I don't think it ever once entered my mind that someone else could win. That was my Bible!

When the Sunday of the contest rolled around, Reverend Courts stepped up to the pulpit to ask if there were any children ready to recite the books of the Bible, but before he could finish speaking, I ran to the front of the church and said them as fast as I could. There was a second's pause and then everyone began applauding and cheering, and Reverend Courts amazed and smiling broadly presented me with my prize. I knew absolutely nothing about that book, but I felt closer to God just holding it in my hand. I had His word! I felt very special!

## A Light in the Valley

Whom shall He teach knowledge? And whom shall He make to understand doctrine? Them that are weaned from the milk and drawn from the breast? For precept must be upon precept, precept upon precept; line upon line, line upon line. Here a little and there a little... Isaiah 28:9&10

Growing up is a lot like a game of hide and seek. Much of what we're looking for is right under our noses where we least expect to find it. Important truths are often hidden under our preconceived notions and uninformed opinions and not until those are stripped away will we really be able to recognize truth. I guess that's why Jesus gave straight ahead instructions on how to get truth: "Ask and it shall be given you; seek, and you shall find; knock and it shall be opened to you." I think many of us are waiting for truth to seek us and knock us down and eliminate the questions and all the effort required in finding the answers and there's no doubt that would be convenient. But would it be valued without effort?

There are many things I've neglected to do in this life either willfully or in ignorance, but those instructions I followed long before I'd ever heard them. I asked, sought, and knocked until I'm sure there were many who because of my importunate questionings, wished me out of sight and hearing!.

If Jesus had not reached for me that day in the backseat of my mothers' car, I've often wondered if I would've ever taken any steps toward Him on my own. My life, like the lives of so many young people was sadly bereft of spiritual leadership. How tragic that so many of us launch out into life and its' crucial decisions without a map, a compass, or even any clear idea as to where we're headed or why we're going at all. We're lost from the very beginning and usually completely unaware of it.

If there's any one thing I've learned, it's that no matter how wretched the situation you're living in, it will come to seem normal if you live in it long enough. It's easy to believe in our own subterfuges and to be comforted with the hackneyed philosophy that the evils of this life are inevitable for everyone and that nothing better or different is to be hoped for. People expect divorce, alcoholism, artifice, lies, greed, hatred, and revenge; they expect kids to go wrong, theft from employees and every other spiritual ill that affects mankind. After all, we tell ourselves, that's just the way it is…that's life. Why should things be any different for me? Or worse still, we compare ourselves to others whose lives are so much more messed up than ours that an easy self-righteousness sets in and we content ourselves with the thought that we must be good because we feed stray cats and dogs, don't rob banks, or kill people and we go to church on Sunday. And in the light of this negative, status quo philosophy we give in without a fight and just get cozy with spiritual mediocrity. Proverbs 29:18 is as succinct a diagnosis of the human condition as can be found anywhere; "Where there is no vision, the people perish."

And so blindness is passed from generation to generation because there are so few real leaders among us. There had been no one leading me to God, and even with the revelation I'd received in the car and my newly acquired Bible there was still something nagging me, something missing that I couldn't put a name to. I had no idea how much more of God there was to know and to have but He was far from finished with me, and more awareness was to be added to that which had already been given.

After those beginning mountaintop experiences, life headed back to the valley of everyday living. My mother tried minimizing my contact with the neighborhood kids. She enrolled me in dance classes, and since I was four years old, she enrolled me in nursery school. I remember being moderately interested in the dance classes, but being a solitary and independent child, I could not always be counted on to conform in social settings.

During my first dance recital I recall being acutely bored, and so I climbed down from the paper Mache' rock on which I was perched in my little fairy costume, and wandered out into the audience and took a seat. No amount of coaxing or knitted eyebrows from my mother or the dance teacher could induce me to return to the stage. But because I eventually came to love dancing, I stayed busy at it for nearly a dozen years and did plenty of performances for which I did stay on stage. As for nursery school, I was expelled in the first month. The incident is fairly clear in my mind, and the few details I was fuzzy on were told again and again in my hearing by the adults who couldn't have forgotten that day even if they'd tried.

It was nap time at the school, and each child was assigned a cot to sleep on. Mine had a stain on it and so I calmly refused to lie down. The teacher, unused to this particular brand of resistance from small people, made an attempt to install me bodily on the cot which didn't work out well at all. The vehemence of my rebellion made it necessary for her to call my mother to come and get me. The teacher felt a need to confine me while she made the call, so I was put into a large walk-in closet. This part I remember very clearly. She turned a light on in the closet and I saw that there were coats hanging up and some purses hanging on the pegs that lined its walls. One capacious and interesting purse hung within reach. It seemed like the most natural thing in the world to ransack the purse which I did in short order, finding a couple of bottles of pills (before the era of childproof caps) that I did not waste any time in opening and sampling. When that poor lady came back to get me out of the closet, I can only imagine the panic she must have felt as she took in the scene. I had eaten one good sized bottle of vitamin pills (without water) and was inspecting the second bottle when she opened the door. I had to be rushed to the doctor as soon as my mother arrived. Needless to say, the nursery school staff felt that it would be better for all concerned if I did not return to school.

As time goes, the year sped by and Kindergarten began for me, and with it the inevitable troubles I would face for years to come. Confrontations occurred with menacing regularity in the neighborhood, and a sort of resignation came over me. It seemed to me that things would never change. I survived each day, and felt lucky if the assaults against me were only verbal. I didn't realize how battle weary I was getting, but then you seldom do when you are only five years old.

It was in this climate of inflexible hatred and rejection that the Lord would shine a spotlight on my heart. After years of persecution the habit of justification settled into my thinking and I came to accept my corresponding attitudes, the rebounding hatred, and the frequent thoughts of revenge that filled my mind concerning my tormentors, and I felt indignant that it should seem wrong to feel those ways. How was I supposed to feel about being shut out of everything, not wanted, and called names...happy? No way! I suppose I was wishing God would *do something* about them. After all, they were in the wrong, not me! But my feelings of being in the wrong persisted, and so to gain a measure of peace, I modified my feelings toward the people who were so hateful to me, but the best I could come up with was simply not to hate them, but I vehemently wished that if they didn't like me, they would just leave me alone! It was being constantly hounded that I could not reconcile myself to. Mentally and emotionally I wrestled against my very active conscience about not being allowed to even think of getting back at these people, who clearly deserved it, but God had already installed a new truth in my heart; you can't hate in peace. I'm sure I had no clear idea that God was at work, I only knew that feelings of hatred and revenge were extremely uncomfortable. I still had a distance to travel to find out that not hating someone was only the first step in pleasing God and simplifying life. Someday, when I was much stronger, I would also be called on to "pray for those who despitefully used me."

Another bit of awareness would be shown to me a couple of years or so later. Usually at school I kept a very low profile in order to deflect some of the unwelcome attention I drew, and over all, this tactic proved to serve me very well. Basically I went through alternate spells of being bullied and tormented, and then forgotten or ignored for brief seasons, which was fine with me. I was violently opposed to anything that disturbed an intermission in *their* attentions to me. There was one particular occasion when my camouflage was suddenly blown, and I was left not only to deal with the renewed assaults of my classmates, but also to find myself face to face with some disconcerting insights into my own heart.

It was time for parent/teacher meetings at the school, and that meant that all the kids and their parents would be attending. In that all black school where I literally had to fight each and every day not to be crushed under the weight of constant disapproval in one form or another, the last thing in the world I wanted to do was be accompanied to my classroom by a white mother. I was absolutely filled with craven terror at being seen with her, and at the same time I felt a searing shame for such disloyal feelings.

In the days leading up to the P.T.A. meeting, dozens of scenarios played out in my mind. I wanted my father to go instead of her since he was black. Fat chance of him getting involved in any domestic event! I wanted to run away and never be heard from again, or get too sick to go; anything rather than be seen with her. I was even angry with her for not understanding how it was with me and not having enough sense to not make it any harder than it already was. However, that dreaded day finally rolled around. I felt physically sick as we drove to the school, and as soon as we were parked and had gotten out of the car, I bolted and put as much distance between us as I could. As soon as the door was opened, I sped down the hallway yelling back to my mother that I needed to go to the bathroom. As young as I was, I knew the instant that I looked back and saw the hurt in her eyes that she understood that I was ashamed to be seen with her. The hurt I saw cut me to the heart.

I was torn between fear of the pain my tormentors were able to inflict on me, and the pain I had just caused someone who didn't deserve it any more than I did. I was full of self-loathing for my cowardly and disloyal feelings, and at the same time I bitterly wondered how else I could be expected to feel under the circumstances. Was it my fault I was hated? Was it my fault I was driven to such desperate behavior? I felt that my lot in life had trapped me into being someone I could hardly approve of. It would be decades before I could put this struggle into the words you now read, but believe me, at the time the feelings were no less potent for not being articulated.

On that day I became aware of a side of myself I'd just as soon not have known about. But you can't fix what you don't realize is broken. So it was a simple P.T.A. meeting that revealed to me the flaws in my own heart which God wanted to mend.

Finally, in 1959 my parents came to the conclusion that it would be better for everyone if we moved to another neighborhood. By now, the hostilities directed at me daily were getting worse, and I knew they were worried that something really serious might happen to me. I know I was. One day when an older girl who hated me more than all the others was chasing me, my mother came outside to confront her and the girl's hatred made her bold enough to even challenge my mother. I also think Earl C. who had a notable temper was worried he might lose it on either the kids or their parents in the event that something did happen to me. Though I knew I would miss our home, I looked forward to the move. I think I believed it might possibly be the end of my troubles.

## Eenie, Meenie, Minie, Moe

The new neighborhood was mostly uninhabited. Indeed, to Earl C. who grew up on the streets of New York, we were truly living in the sticks. Our home, which had just been built, was only the third house on that block! The several streets that made up the neighborhood were also very sparsely populated; a house or two in each block. Eventually the neighborhood would fill up with newly built homes, but for now it was a wilderness of peace for me. There were lots of fields and trees, and in sheer bliss I wandered around my new domain free from harassment for the first time in my young life. There were absolutely no words for the gratitude and contentment I felt in this unimaginable dispensation of rest!

In this interval of personal refreshment my thoughts turned once again to God. My daily delight with the wind and sky, and beautiful fields was more than enough compensation for the remaining discord in my life, and gave me the opportunity to think my own thoughts which in turn gave me new strength to carry the problems in my life that would be with me a long time. I'd always loved the out-of-doors since my early introduction to Medicine Acres, but in my old neighborhood I'd seldom had the freedom to enjoy it because I was always either on the lookout for, or running from trouble. My school situation remained the same as did my peculiar family life, but now I had the tranquility of my newly entrenched solitude which I depended on more than I knew to counter-balance the rest of my troubles. I was a regular little pantheist. I felt closest to God when I could see the sky and hear the wind and to that end I strove to be outside with the beauty of creation. I was generally irritable when for any reason I had to be indoors for too long. Some things never change, and to this day I am still as enchanted with the out-of-doors as I ever was and it is still just as disagreeable as when I was a child to have any business which keeps me away from the sky too long.

Not long after we moved to our new home, a girl named Patsy who I'd met and spent some time with in the old neighborhood moved a block away from us with her mother and brother. She was to be my best friend throughout the school years and the sister I'd never had. We did everything together. When she was not spending the night at my house, I was spending it at hers. We took violin lessons together, dance lessons, bought matching clothes and glasses, and roamed the city streets on bikes or afoot. I even went with her family to the 1964 World's Fair in New York City. I owe much to her mother Mrs. B., who did not forebear to instruct me, feed me, and look out for me over the years with the same zeal with which she raised her own children. She was a schoolteacher and it seemed to me that nothing ever escaped her attention. She had an enviable character and was a huge presence in my life. Next to my grandmother, she and Mrs. Courts whom I still saw from time to time were the people I most admired and respected.

Though I'd never been popular, Patsy was, and undoubtedly her popularity had a positive effect on the view the rest of the neighborhood took of me. As a result of her unspoken endorsement, over time there were other children in whose homes I spent many pleasant afternoons. As time went on, my oppressors were more snide and covert in their persecutions, and most of that took place at school, hardly ever in the neighborhood.

But by now, a pattern had been set in my life from earlier years that would remain with me to the end…that of seeking solitude. Now and then some kid would come to the door to see if I wanted to do something, but most of the time I chose to be alone with my books and music, and with the sky. Solitude had become the asylum that more often than not won out even over my occasional desire for companionship. Being tolerated instead of actively persecuted is still not the same thing as being accepted and wanted, and anything short of a total connection was for me not worth the effort.

In one thing I was almost the same as any other young girl, and that was the inevitable elementary and junior high school romances. I say almost because my choice of boyfriends was a head scratching mystery to my parents and friends. They were a most unlikely collection for sure. But I always saw (or thought I saw) something in them that was completely unrecognized by anyone but me. One thing they all seemed to have in common was that they were underdogs; the ones considered by the rest of the school crowd to be losers. They were comprised of boys too shy, too dark, not a part of the in crowd, or just too homely. I was constantly being grilled as to what in the world I saw in them! Looking back, I was still knocked off my feet by each one in turn and have no regrets for those early choices. Patsy's brother,

Bobby, would always shake his head and say "Well, at least she doesn't think she's too good for anybody." In retrospect maybe I was just trying to extend to them the acceptance that I had been denied. Sometimes I wonder what became of all the old beaus I'd seen such wonderful things in. I always believed in them the way I wanted to be believed in.

One boyfriend in particular from my elementary and junior high school days that I would like to raise a tribute to, since in my eyes he died a hero at seventeen, was a boy named Larry Barry He was in the same dance classes as Patsy and me for several years. In fact, many of our dance school's tap dance routines were built around the three of us.

He was a vibrant young person of integrity from a close and wonderful Christian family. Our relationship and dance connection lasted from elementary school to the time of his death which was brought about when after school one day on his way home, he saw a girl being threatened and physically assaulted on her porch by her boyfriend. True to his gentlemanly nature, he intervened to protect her from harm and was knifed by the boyfriend and died hours later. He may not have been considered especially handsome by the majority of kids which wasn't so much because he was not good looking as that he was very dark-skinned, but I liked his dark skin, and his sincerity and congeniality made him extraordinarily handsome and special to me. When he died, I felt a great good had gone out of the world.

Meanwhile, amidst the turmoil's of youth, since I was still only allowed to go to churches within walking distance, I decided to go to a Methodist church two blocks from my house. It was a lot different, and to me less friendly than Rev. Courts' church in my old neighborhood. I missed the services and most of all Rev. and Mrs. Courts very much, but there was nothing to do but give this new church a chance. It was a large church with an older congregation of very somber saints. The only real attraction I found in going there was the children's choir which was under the direction of a kindly older woman named Sister Griffin.

Every Saturday we had choir rehearsal, and Sister Griffin would always have treats for us afterward. I think I'd have felt a little more warmly towards her, except that she had a disconcerting predilection for discussing her soon coming funeral with a fervor that children find hard to relate to. She would get this wistful look in her eyes as she told us about the songs she wanted sung when the Lord called her home and of the flowers she hoped would adorn her casket. We could understand getting excited over an upcoming birthday party or special trip, but to look forward to death and funerals was not only spooky, it was beyond us. Besides, she seemed awfully healthy to be so preoccupied with dying. Apart from her curious mindset, we were very fond of her, and she was always good to us.

The church however, did not satisfy me. Nothing was happening. There was an odd sense of death according to a child's perception in that place. I've often wondered if had anything to do with the fact that it was in that church that I'd attended my first funeral and the first time I'd ever seen a dead person, which haunted my imagination for days. But as time went by, I knew it was something deeper. I once remember going to the cemetery with my mother and grandmother who'd gone to place flowers on the graves of the family's departed, and images of life underground and other nondescript misconceptions of death flared in my young, over imaginative head. But the overall feeling was one of stagnation and of being weighed down. That was how it felt in that church to me. After my introduction to God in the backseat of my mother's car, and the winning of my little Bible, this was definitely anticlimactic. I wanted something more.

It wasn't long before the area we'd moved to filled up with neighbors. Among them were two families that would introduce me to other spiritual possibilities. One family lived just across the street and had two daughters, one a year younger, one a year older than me. The other family lived down the block a ways with a son and a daughter not much younger than me. It turned out that both families had known each other a long time since they belonged to the same Catholic Church, and the children all attended St.

Matthews Catholic school together. The fact that their school was a part of their church, and that they learned things about God everyday sounded exactly like what I was looking for. Then too, they had these important looking (at least to me) uniforms that they wore to school. Of course, they hated them, but I was thoroughly impressed. Surely in a school where children studied things about God I would be safe from name calling and confrontations. I was pretty sure I needed to go to a Catholic school and dress in uniforms and I wasted no time in my campaign to convince my parents of it. I tormented my mother daily. I think she saw my side of it and might have given in if she could have convinced my father about the matter of tuition.

My friendship with the new kids progressed nicely, and in due time I was invited to go with their family to Mass on Sunday. This church was farther away than any of the ones I was used to going to, but I was allowed to go because their parents were going, and then too, I felt my mother was trying in her way to make amends to me for my disappointment at not being allowed to go to the Catholic school.

Though I was too excited to sleep much the night before church, I was up bright and early, anxious to be ready in time to leave. Once my mother was satisfied with my appearance and I'd gotten off the hook from eating breakfast, I crossed the street to meet them at their house. The girls came out beautifully dressed, but wonders never cease, they each had a white lace doily on top of their head. That was to be the first of a succession of novelties for me that morning.

Once we arrived at church and passed through the arched doorway into the vestibule, I saw that there were little bowls attached to the walls which I later discovered contained what was called holy water, whatever that meant. Everyone dipped in a finger and then traced the sign of the cross; forehead to solar plexus; shoulder to shoulder. Feeling that it was not the most appropriate time, I saved my thousand questions for later and quickly adopted the human doctrine; "When in Rome..." (No pun intended). Whatever I saw them do, I did.

As the service started there was a sense of high ceremony. Candles were lighted by young boys dressed in long robes who could not have been any older than me. They and the priest, Father as he was called, also impressively dressed, walked slowly up the aisle as though they were in a wedding. I watched every move with evolving anticipation. Once the priest began to speak, it was in a language that I'd never heard before. First he spoke; then the entire congregation responded in the same strange tongue. I was completely swept away. It seemed that the mysteries of God were almost palpable. In that place, I felt on the verge of discovery. I felt excitement and expectancy. Everything about it seemed beautiful to me and I felt sure this must be the real thing; the thing I'd been looking for my whole life! My heart and mind embraced all that I saw and heard and I felt a rush of gratitude to my neighbors for inviting me to this wonderful place. Hey, I could wear a doily on my head, and hold the mysterious rosary beads in my hands and memorize the prayers that went with each bead! I could dip my hands in the holy water and learn to speak another language! All the ceremony of service with priests in regal attire, the season of Lent and its sacrifices, confession, catechism, no meat on Fridays, all had a feeling of sacredness; a feeling of holiness that drew me in. I felt like my search was over!

After I'd attended a few of their services, I was allowed to go to catechism twice a week after school with my new friends. There were also lots of Catholic children at my school and it was with them that I walked to the church for catechism after school. This extra time of indoctrination had the same special feeling as being initiated into a club; of being a part of something important.

Catechism took place at the local parish and usually when it was over the kids hung around to talk for a while, but I was always drawn to the sanctuary and so I would sneak away unnoticed. Closing the door quietly behind me, I would creep in awe down the aisle of the sanctuary; just to see the candles burning and to look on all the saintly faces in paintings hanging on the walls, and the statues of the different saints; all these ancient looking artifacts stirred up great curiosity in my impressionable and hungry heart.

There was one room in particular that I couldn't keep away from. In the back of the sanctuary, to the left of the entrance doors, was a small room always in semi-gloom. Inside, and taking up almost the whole room was a stone slab. On it was a life size statue of the crucified Christ. His hands and feet were pierced through, and a gaping wound was in His side, and His blood seemed to stream onto the slab. He lay on the slab as though brought there straight from the cross. Candles burned all around Him, and on each side of Him running the length of the slab were benches on which to kneel and pray. On my knees there beside Jesus was the main attraction of the Catholic Church for me. Though it filled me with sorrow for what had happened to Him, I just had to be there; to somehow associate myself with His suffering. He looked so real lying there, that it seemed I could just reach out my hand and touch His flesh; that at any moment He would wake up and look at me. I hoped that somehow He knew I was there with Him. I spent a lot of time in that little room with feelings strange and wonderful; just wanting to be near Him, and wishing very much that He was alive and I could know Him.

I kept going to Mass and catechism for a few months still waiting for something more to happen, when during one of the lessons I overheard one of the sisters say to a child standing near me that people who were not Catholics were going to hell. Young as I was, I felt instant anger at that woman, and was sure beyond a doubt that what she said was not true; that Jesus lying on the slab bleeding in the front vestibule didn't feel that way at all. What made her think she knew what God was going to do with people? That indignation abruptly ended my interest in the Catholic Church. It would be many years before I would darken their door again.

The circumstances that brought about my next spiritual move aren't quite clear in my memory, but seem to have been prompted by a music program that Patsy's mother had heard about. Whatever the reason, I was once again among the Baptists. Well, most of the time. Since I spent a fair amount of time in Jackson, MI visiting my grandmother (who also did not attend church) and I was bound by the same rules I had to follow at home; I could only attend churches within walking distance. In this case it was a Mormon church. They all seemed pleased to have me, and were very kind, but I had the sense of it being more of a community gathering together to encourage and fellowship with one another, rather than the seeking or worshipping of God or of studying His word. There was absolutely no fire there either, but I continued back and forth between the Baptists and the Mormons for a season. Of course, the humor of this situation was lost on me at the time. Perhaps the Baptists and the Mormons, had they known of my dual participation would have taken me aside to enlighten me. Maybe I was just so used to the *mixed* situations in race, that *mixed* spiritual experiences didn't seem all that strange to me.

More and more often my thoughts hungrily returned to the little church I'd grown up across the street from where the people danced and shouted and shook tambourines late into the night. If only...

I guess it would be easy for someone to say I was just longing for the proverbial greener pasture, but I still believe that God was using my hunger to point me in the direction that would eventually lead me to what I was looking for. For the time being, I was too young to over-ride adult decisions made on my behalf, but someday the choice would be mine.

Most young folks are equipped with adjustable dispositions when it comes to adapting to their parents' mandates. You get over it, and go on and do that which is allowed if you know what's good for you. True to my species, I didn't spend a lot of time stewing about Harris Temple though it crossed my mind frequently, but instead jumped into the new Baptist church whole heartedly; MT. Olive it was called.

Every Sunday morning, Patsy and I would head for services there. Usually either my father or her mother took us and picked us up, except in fine weather we would walk the three mile round trip just for the pleasure of it. In due time I was baptized--again. One thing's for sure, if baptism was the only requirement in the plan of salvation, there's no doubt that I was well covered since I'd been baptized in almost every denomination known to man before it was all over. I thought perhaps now I had found my church home. Most of the people seemed pleasant, and there were many things to hold my attention, at least for a while.

There was a really cool choir director, a young guy who was actually quite a noteworthy vocalist. He had lots of energy, ideas, and charisma. There was also an element of the miraculous about him. Though he seemed perfect to us, he was plagued by a horrific stutter. The miraculous part was that while he stuttered at almost every spoken syllable, he never stuttered while singing.

I had quite a crush on him (as did several of the other girls in the choir) and was transported to the pinnacle of adolescent romanticism when the director himself chose me to sing a duet with him; and not just any song, but my favorite song at that time, from my favorite movie; West Side Story. The song was "One Hand, One Heart"; the love song of all love songs sung by the story's own lovers. Add that together with my crush on him and you have rich materials for the spinning of daydreams for months to come, and daydream material is of monumental importance in solitude. And so, for the moment, it seemed I'd found a place to be. Unbeknownst to me, I was already diverted from my main objective, even though sweetly so. Because there are so many colorful side events such as this in any church, it's possible to get totally wrapped up in them, which in themselves are harmless, but don't necessarily get you any closer to God. The search for God is totally on the seeker. He's always around; we're the ones who get side-tracked from time to time.

Still, this church was pretty exciting and it was still early. Just maybe what I was looking for would happen. Sometimes I think I was waiting to be hijacked by God. It would have helped a lot if I'd had the slightest idea what I was looking for. But all that was a long way off and I was still hungrily feeling around in the dark as it were.

One scary but very interesting thing happened during my stay at MT Olive that I would never lose sight of in my search for God. There was a woman who was always at church whose face I remember only vaguely, her name not at all. I think these facts were eclipsed in my mind by two outstanding features connected with her. She frequently wore a mink stole that sent a shiver through me every time I saw her in it. It was one of those deals where the mink's heads were left on, and it appeared that they were biting each other's' tails in order to stay connected around her tiny self. Their shiny little dried up eyes and noses were distinctly creepy, and more than a little morbid to me. It was a wonder to me how she could stand to wear it.

But there was something else about her; something that captivated my attention even more than her scary coat. Sometimes in service she would get so carried away with what the preacher was preaching that she would *get happy*. That's what everybody said was happening to her; *gettin' happy*. She would start out moaning softly, calling out Jesus' name, eyes closed, rocking back and forth, completely oblivious to anything; lost in what she was experiencing. Finally, her worship would reach a crescendo and she would jump up out of her seat and shout, throwing the infamous and dreaded mink in all directions. Almost as soon as she began this uninhibited worship, the ushers and deacons all dressed in crisp, white uniforms would come and speak gently to her and either escort or carry her (according to the intensity of her outburst) out into the vestibule until she could get control of herself. At that point, the preacher's voice was lost to me as my eyes and concentration were on the woman on the other side of the glass doors just behind the pew I was sitting in. still completely enraptured in worship while the deacons fanned her, talked soothingly and tried to get her to drink a little water.

Looking back, it sort of felt like the same scenario you'd imagine in a mental hospital with doctors and nurses trying to subdue a raving patient. Everyone seemed slightly embarrassed by these episodes, except her, who seemed greatly refreshed afterwards. But I remember being devoutly interested in what was happening to her and secretly wished that it would happen to me so that I would know what she'd felt. There was definitely the recurrent thought that just maybe she was on to something the rest of us were missing. She was sweet and kind and seemed perfectly normal when she wasn't having a spell, so I felt pretty sure she wasn't crazy. I wanted very much to ply her with questions, but child/adult relations were quite different then, and you just didn't approach grown-ups and blatantly ask them about the reasons for their behavior.

What on earth (or in Heaven) was causing her to behave that way? It seems strange to consider from my present vantage point that she might have been the only person I had seen in any church thus far in my searching who'd had a real relationship with God.

As for me, I felt like I'd traveled a long way, but hadn't gotten very far; I was still hungry and thirsty. Since that far away day in the backseat of my mothers' car when I had come to know that God really is, I had longed for some kind of communion with Him. I believed beyond a doubt that He really exists and always sees me, and yet I felt an abyss of silence between us.

I had gone to the places where I was told I would find Him, but He wasn't there; not so that I could talk to Him; not so that I could hear Him; not so that I could feel His love. It was very frustrating, but I was compelled to continue my search. If I had known that it would be another fifteen years of groping in the dark; of pitfalls so deep that only now do I see that if He had not kept me there would have been no surviving them.; and of mistakes made in the darkness, of ignorance that would send me on perilous, soul sapping detours, that unless an unseen hand had caught me, I would surely have hit the bottom and not come up. But Jesus had faith in me before I had faith in Him, and so I was compelled to continue my journey one day at a time, not then realizing that with every step, I was getting closer.

# Chapter 1

## PART 2

# Consequences of Solitude

# A Detour

By the time I started junior high, it looked to me like I'd achieved about all the connection I was going to get out of this world which drew a disconsolate sigh from my soul. Troubles at school had diminished to tolerable proportions. Though I was still generally disliked and talked about by some, and ignored by the rest, physical violence was past; usually more a threat than an actuality. I still had Patsy's friendship, but was just as much at odds with my parents as I had ever been. Church was a good habit and I made sure I always went, but even there, I felt like I had come to a dead-end without finding whatever it was I was after.

It was during this time of life-in-limbo that I wished more than ever for a brother or sister or someone to be a part of. It was an aching need that never lightened. My home life seemed empty with no one to share a core family existence with, when seemingly out of the blue came Kent J., whom I had first noticed when I began junior high school; a boy that I really liked who paid me a lot of attention; not boyfriend type attention, but just a curious lingering sort of interest. He started to walk me home from school each day, never talking very much, but just seeming to want to be with me. He was a shy type and didn't hang out with many kids at school. A lot of the girls at school thought him good looking, but he didn't seem to notice or care much. He always came in when we got home and generally stayed a couple of hours or more almost every evening. I felt it was a bit strange that there was neither surprise nor curiosity from my parents that he was there. He was quiet, but very polite.

His presence confused me and I thought it odd that I was allowed to spend so much time alone with a boy two years older than me. Ordinarily, Earl C. would've raised sand even if he'd been one of the twelve disciples. Most of the time we listened to music, or talked about some of the kids we knew at school. Kent was somewhat cagy during my artless interrogations regarding him personally, so I backed off and just accepted the relationship for what it was. Since my mother bred dogs as one of her myriad long term projects and he was very knowledgeable about them, especially their grooming, he spent considerable time teaching me the different cuts for the long haired breeds until eventually I got pretty good at it. A few years after he graduated he moved to California and set up a pet grooming salon in Hollywood where he groomed many celebrities' pets. Thus ended my time with him which I missed very much.

It wasn't until I graduated from high school that I learned that Kent was my brother; John's son. My mother had traded his right to see me for his silence about his identity. I had a lot of trouble to forgive her over that. I always felt she'd stolen him from me. How much more I would have treasured those times of ours if I'd known he was my brother.

It was shortly after this era, about ninth grade, that Patsy and I, ever loyal to our favorite recreation of roller skating and never missing a chance to go that a new connection was ushered into my life. Stewart School, where we'd gone to elementary school still had skating on Wednesday nights and we were as faithful to that as to church. It was the place to go to catch up on any good gossip, to see and be seen, and most of all to flirt and capture the interest of the boys in our neighborhood.

There were all levels of skating represented there; the *baby* skaters who had to stay near the middle where they could skate slowly and fall down in peace without being run over by the more advanced skaters, and the *Pros* who were whistle blowing floor guards and could skate at top speed forward and backwards. Patsy and I fell somewhere in the middle. Our faithfulness had made us fairly proficient skaters. Besides music, going to the show, and dancing, skating was an event we rarely missed.

Not everyone came to skate. Wednesday night skating was plagued with visitations from the local *bad boys* who were much older but condescended to drop in, show off, and check out the young girls…give 'em a thrill. So they came and hung out against the walls calling out flirtatious remarks to get the attention of the girls skating by. The girls giggled and pointed and whispered to each other which of course, tweaked their vanity and encouraged them to even bolder conduct. There was avid curiosity about the myths surrounding the handsome young boys that our mamas called thugs, but because of the way they just showed up and effortlessly dominated the atmosphere so unlike any of the shy and backwards boys of our own age group, there was a general consensus among us that perhaps our mamas just didn't know what was going on.

One boy in particular singled me out and began to try to coax me from the floor every time I skated by. I was mostly afraid of him but I didn't want him to know that, and I didn't want to appear rude or stuck up by not speaking and of course I was flattered by his attention and curious about this as-of-yet unknown species of boy. I would have been well within my rights to have completely ignored him, but I didn't quite know how to, so I consented to sit with him on the bleachers and talk. After all, I told myself, it can't hurt to talk a minute with all these people around, and I'll just tell him I can't talk to him after this. His Name was Phillip.

He was very tall and good looking; in fact the best looking guy in the crowd. I didn't realize what a highly coveted prize he was considered to be in the circle of older girls who glared at me in jealousy. All the kids my own age were watching me with a mixture of awe and apprehension such as would be expressed if someone we knew decided to have lunch with either a celebrity or an ex-con. Since for the most part I was a loner, I was oblivious to the reputation of the guy now sitting next to me, but everyone else seemed to know a lot about him. I was now the center of attention in a much different way than what I was used to. His manner to my way of thinking was very extravagant. During that same time frame I used to watch Cassius Clay, now the estimable Mohammed Ali, fight and I marveled at his arrogant boasting and wild self-assurance, and this boys' arrogance was exactly the same brand of swagger.

But he wasn't rude as I had imagined he might be. His manners were nice; he had a job as an electrician with his father's company, and a shiny new car which to me was extremely impressive for someone his age. The more he talked, the more fascinated I became. I was terribly intimidated by him partly because he was almost five years older than me. One got the feeling that he didn't play by the rules; that maybe he had the capacity even for being dangerous. But I had the generous spirit of the naive and felt that he couldn't possibly be as bad as people made him out to be. Part of my reasoning came from my personal experience with rumors; certainly people had said awful things about me all my life that weren't true. Perhaps he had gone through the same injustices I had. I felt a little sorry for him, a feeling he would've probably found amusing if he'd been aware of it.

He asked if he could drive me home when skating was over and since I had never been in any boy's car, I didn't dare say yes without calling home first and asking even though it was only half a mile home from the school. I received a clear warning from Patsy's eyes, but I just let it roll off and called home anyway. I could tell on the phone that my folks weren't knocked out about it, but they reluctantly gave their permission. The ride home felt strange and I was pressed against the passenger door as though I might jump out if he so much as sneezed. This seemed to be more amusing to him than offensive and I could see his lips twitch as if to suppress a smile. We made it to my house in less than three minutes and then he came in to meet my parents.

The next day at school the embellished word was out about my ride home with the notorious bad boy Philip H. Really…I felt like I'd done something illegal! I was hit with all sorts of unsolicited advice about how to handle the situation. "In the first place", said the majority of the girls "he's just messin' with you. You ain't gonna be able to keep him. So and so's been after him and they used to date, and she's older and got more goin' on than you." And the guys were saying "Better watch out! Get yourself in trouble hangin' out with him." Little did I realize the same thing was happening to him with his home boys. "Man, you can't go out with her. She's one of them goody-good girls and she's under the limit and you a thug out here in the streets brotha. Besides, her father'll kill you. Better cut that loose"

You might say we were sort of dared into a relationship. Tell a teenager what they can't do or can't have and it skyrockets to the head of the priority list of must-haves. There was on both sides an attraction to be sure, but I think all the outside prophesying on both sides about the unlikelihood of our being able to succeed together gave it just the right spice to make it more appealing than it probably would have been if it had been left alone.

Sure enough, he came by the next day, and the next, and then to skating again where he asked me to *go with him*. Now that we were an official item, I thought that would be the end of that. Not so. I began to get all kinds of menacing phone calls from old girlfriends and wanna-be girlfriends who felt that physical assault was the perfect answer to getting rid of me and gaining his interest. At first these older girls really frightened me, and then I became annoyed, and finally very angry.

I was pretty standoffish for a girlfriend since I'd never gotten over feeling intimidated by him. He probably took it as a sign that I wouldn't be too difficult a conquest. After a couple of weeks, he began pressuring me for sex and taunting me with the girls who were always calling him; telling me how they would do whatever he wanted. All he had to do was ask, and I knew it was true. I might have been tempted to give in if I'd felt any genuine affection for him, but as it was my feelings were mostly fascination tinged with fear. Like all the kids I knew, I'd been taught sex before marriage was wrong, so I stubbornly held on to my convictions for several more months in spite of his quarrelling, importuning, and threatening to leave me to go out with one of the other girls. I continually wondered why he spent so much energy on challenging me instead of carrying out his threats. If I'd been possessed of a little wisdom I could have seen that he was pleasantly impressed in some strange way that he hadn't been able to persuade me to do what I knew was wrong, but I was too young to realize the power in holding on to your ideals and principles. Our relationship was more of a contest of wills than a romance. I would have broken up with him if I'd know how to. Youth is a strange thing. No adult in their right mind would hang on to a relationship where there was so little common ground to stand on.

In the middle of my emotional turmoil, Patsy's brother, Bobby, had a friend that was very interested in me. He was the same age as Phillip, really good looking and I liked him a lot, and more importantly there was nothing dark or intimidating about him. I preferred him hands down to Phillip. He was constantly pestering Bobby and Patsy's mother to intercede for him with my parents to see if he would be allowed to come and visit me. One evening the phone rang and it was Mrs. Booker calling to see if Bill could call on me. My folks agreed and he actually came to see me a few times. I enjoyed his company very much; easy conversation and laughter flowed between us, but the whole situation grated on Earl C. unendurably. Though he would never have admitted it openly, he would rather I went out with a black bad boy than any kind of white boy which I thought the zenith of unfairness since he had married my mother. But to my extreme disappointment, he forbade Bill to come by anymore; Phillip was back, and trouble was coming.

I wish at this juncture of my life I would have had more self-esteem, wisdom, or even outright rebellion, but the truth was that even though I was aware of some alarming characteristics in Phillip, I didn't know how to disengage myself from the relationship. I was actually too afraid of him to break up. I wished very much that my parents would've monitored my association with this troubled young man a little more closely, but my relationship with them had never been what you'd call close or open. I just wasn't in the habit of talking to anyone about things that really bothered me. I was angry that my father didn't get rid of Phillip instead of Bill. I didn't even confide to Patsy about my confusion and feelings of helplessness in coping with Phillip or how much I really liked and preferred Bill.

In hindsight I feel my parents left me in a vulnerable position by allowing Phillip to visit me at home even when they weren't going to be there. They seemed to trust him though I couldn't for the life of me figure out why. Between his constant importuning and my parents' absence from home during many of his visits, I finally made the wrong decision and ended up pregnant. It was early July, a mere two months after my sixteenth birthday.

Unlike most girls who found themselves dealing with teenage pregnancy, I was neither worried nor frantic. I was secretly ecstatic. It had nothing whatsoever to do with Phillip…it was all about the baby. Certainly my feelings about this untimely pregnancy were not what anyone could call normal, but they were definitely shaped by the solitude I'd known since early childhood and my deep longing for a real connection. The way I saw it was that now at last I would have someone who would belong to me, and I would belong to them; we would love each other. I hadn't been able to love my adoptive parents, and though they took care of me and made a life for me, I didn't feel much love from them either. This was the answer to my problem! I was as happy as if I'd had good sense. It never once crossed my mind to add Phillip to this equation. I didn't dream of marrying him or of being together forever and us having a family as other girls in my situation did. I just wanted it to be me and the baby.

As soon as my mother suspected my pregnancy, she confronted me in a storm of tears and was frankly baffled that I was not at all upset over it. What I hadn't counted on was what my parents were going to require of me in my dilemma. My thoughts had only encompassed me and the coming baby. Now my parents who were very old fashioned about such things were talking about me getting married! That was the first time frantic ever got hold of me. I was totally okay with having a child out of wedlock and caring for it. I was too accustomed to the disapproval of others for it to have any power over me at this late date. But the thought of marrying Phillip hadn't even crossed my mind and was absolutely abhorrent to me! *That*, I wanted no part of! He frightened me often with his cruelty and he had a violent streak that I later understood to be the anger and frustration he felt over the unsatisfactory relationship between him and his father.

The thought of living alone with him day after day filled me with sick dread. I felt I could deal with one problem, but had no desire to undertake the second mistake which I deeply felt that marriage to him would be. I said as much to my parents, but my mothers' main concern was that if we didn't marry soon everyone would know that the baby was conceived before the wedding, which I thought was just crazy. It was truly generational. I felt that marriage at sixteen was more or less a statement that there was already a baby. Who would get married that young unless they felt they had to? And while I wasn't afraid to have the baby, I was terrified of getting married. I resisted my parents on this point, but they were unmovable; either I would get married, or I would have to have an abortion. Abortions were not legal in Michigan at the time, so that would've meant a trip to New York or some other costly arrangement. This option was even more horrifying than getting married and struck real fear into my heart. I felt that I absolutely could not part with this baby that I wanted so desperately.

After a few more days of wrangling with my folks, I finally consented to marry Phillip. Curiously, he seemed quite happy with this arrangement; my father was grim but appeased; my mother however, was devastated. She'd had such big plans for my future. She had spent a small fortune during the last decade on singing lessons, dance lessons, violin lessons, horseback riding lessons, modeling, baton twirling and piano lessons, all so I could be something great, and now to her it just all seemed wasted. For her, an acceptable gratitude would have been for me to have become famous. It was what she wanted most. And now, to her, all I would be was another Shirley which opinion she did not spare me.

One very small consolation was that my mother got to plan the wedding. She loved to arrange events like that though her opportunities were few. I didn't involve myself at all with the wedding plans since it was the last thing I wanted to do. I had zero interest in being married and even had I been deeply in love and looking forward to it, my idea of a wedding would have been simplicity at its finest. I didn't even choose my wedding dress, but somehow everything got done and then suddenly it was time to do the undoable.

It seems a crying shame that I should have such a fuzzy recollection of a day that by rights ought to have been one of the most important and happiest days of my life and every moment cherished to furnish old age with the joy of precious memories. I don't even remember the exact date; only that it was early September. But the truth was, the marriage was to me a farce and an emotional lie from which I could draw no comfort. The secret wellspring of my joy was the baby that would soon be not ours, but mine.

After the wedding and reception which was attended by family, schoolmates, and the neighborhood, we left immediately for Ann Arbor, Michigan where Phillip and his father were working most of the time. His father was an electrical contractor who owned his own company; Phillip was a journeyman electrician and at the time of our marriage they were in the middle of wiring some apartments there. We moved into the apartment he had already been living in.

I felt as though I were on a space ship to another planet as our car pulled out of my parents' driveway crammed with wedding gifts. My mother looked grey with disappointment as she waved good-bye and I felt sad that the days and weeks ahead would probably be hard for her. This parting sight and the thought of being separated from Patsy and everything familiar wasn't tempered by the joy of starting a new life with someone loved and trusted. It was one of the emptiest feelings I'd yet felt. The only thing that made these frightening sacrifices even remotely tolerable was the coming baby.

Due to the graphic horrors and negativity of this period of my life, my story here will be greatly abbreviated. A sketch is somewhat necessary to understand the degree of solitude that followed me into what should have been a place of love and companionship. But the brutality I experienced only served to take solitude to a whole new dimension.

Being newlyweds we didn't have a lot of belongings to start life with and so our apartment was easily and speedily put into order. We were married on Friday; settled by Saturday afternoon, and he went back to work Monday morning. There was no honeymoon. It was that Monday morning that began what would be for me a long and extremely perilous stay in Ann Arbor, Michigan.

Back when I'd been contesting marriage to Phillip with my parents the issue of my continuing school came up. Phillip thought I should drop out which I emphatically refused to do. My parents backed me on this point and so Phillip capitulated and it was decided I would continue my education at Pioneer High in Ann Arbor.

On this Monday morning, three days after my wedding, I was preparing to go to the school to register when all hell broke out. Phillip informed me that now that he was my husband, he was also my boss. There would be no school. I became very angry in turn. It had already been decided; he'd promised my parents and me that my education would not be interrupted. To my obviously hurt and querulous inquiry into this blatant deception he laughed and asked how the hell I thought I was going to get there. Besides, I didn't need to go to school. Things were different now. My parents weren't around and there was nothing I could do about it, besides he was going to work and I would not be allowed to use the car *ever*! I wanted to call my parents on the phone to find out what I should do, but he had already decided (minus my input) that he wasn't going to have a phone in our apartment, and there were no cell phones at that time. The only phone was in his fathers' apartment on the other side of the apartment complex. His father was not a man easily entreated for any purpose and so unless it had been a matter of life and death I would avoid him as long as I could. Besides, how could I talk to my parents freely in front of him about my problems with his son? I must have looked hurt and betrayed standing there trying to hold Phillip to his promise. He seemed highly pleased at my helpless consternation, laughed at me in my predicament and left for work.

There was nothing at the moment that I could do, but I felt determined that it wouldn't be the end of the matter. I had to think even though I felt completely overwhelmed. There was absolutely no one for me to turn to. I didn't have one friend in Ann Arbor; no connections at the school, no phone to call around to find out anything, no car to go anywhere in, and no money of my own…nothing. I felt trapped and completely at the mercy of someone who was enjoying the fact that I felt that way. The only person I knew was Phillip's father and I was more afraid of him than I was of Phillip. He was a grouchy, unapproachable, unemotional workaholic who thought our whole situation was a bunch of nonsense that had interfered with his work schedule and he was highly displeased with Phillip who danced attendance to try to please him.

After these dreary assessments I hardly knew how to proceed. At last I decided that the only thing I could do was to go out and find a phone book, not that I had any money to make a call, and try to find out where exactly the school was. And so I set out walking and went into a nearby drugstore that let me use their phonebook. Once I had the school's address, I asked for directions explaining that I was new and didn't know where anything was. It turned out that Pioneer high was a little more than three miles away from where I lived. I quickly wrote down the directions so that I could memorize the street names. There wouldn't be time enough today for me to walk there and get back before Phillip got home from work and it would probably be too late to register today anyway, so I headed back to the apartment.

Among the wedding gifts I'd received was a tiny Siamese kitten which Philip had given me. I named her Beebee and loved her instantly. When I came in from my excursion to gather information about the city, Phillip was home unexpectedly early and my kitten was having some species of fit running around the apartment screeching and rubbing its' watering eyes with its paws. I quickly found out the reason for it; Phillip had put pepper in her eyes and some type of sore muscle remedy like Heat on its' rear end and was delightedly enjoying the results.

I felt physically ill as it dawned on me that I was dealing much more closely than I was prepared for, with someone who was not only mentally unbalanced, but who also had a penchant for cruelty the likes of which I couldn't even imagine existed. Into the bargain, he was six feet two inches of brute strength which of course, I was no match for. A sort of terror came over me that this stranger I was looking at was capable of unbelievable mental and physical cruelty and there was no one for me to go to for help.

I washed out my kitten's eyes the best I could while trying to control my tears and my fury which I felt could only get us into more trouble if detected. I heard him laughing and asking what I thought I was going to do about it. I didn't answer. Suddenly suspicious, he asked me where I'd been to which I answered that I'd only been out walking around the complex to get a little air.

Luckily, his work schedule began early in the morning. He was up at five a.m. and usually gone by six; plenty of time for me to get to the school. Since he never got home before five in the afternoon, I had an excellent chance of being home long before he would get there. It wasn't that I thought I could go to school without him knowing, but I definitely wanted to make the initial connection without his knowledge. Somehow, there had to be someone else in this city that I could make aware of my presence. I guess I thought at least if I were in school, if for some reason I didn't show up, there would be someone to check up on me.

Over the course of the next four months, I became reasonably familiar with my end of town since I had to walk the nearly seven miles round trip to school and back every day, and I learned to really love Ann Arbor apart from my painful marriage. There were many interesting places that I sometimes stopped into on my way home, and the kindness and openness of people certainly helped a little, although I never made any kind of connection where I felt I could share the types of problems I had. Sure enough, as soon as Phillip knew he had been overridden on the school issue he became ugly indeed. He remained firm about my not being able to use the car or of taking me to school. That was out of the question!

There was nothing I could do or say that didn't precipitate an argument or bring on jeering criticism from Phillip. I learned not to say much and to keep away from him even in our apartment. I was continually afraid for my safety and that of my little kitten. All of my life I'd grown up with pets around and in our family they were not only treated responsibly, they were downright spoiled members of the family. My father may have gotten drunk and terrorized my mother and me, but I never recalled a single incident when he kicked the dog. It was this cruelty to a helpless animal that made me feel like I was in the presence of pure evil.

Ann Arbor schools were not like Flint schools. It was more like going to college. There was no seating arrangement that had to be adhered to, and many of the classrooms were trailers situated around the campus of Pioneer High. One rule that was the same as in any other high school at that time was that if you were pregnant, you could not attend.

My mother had bought me a coat before I'd left for Ann Arbor that was more like a cape to hide my increasing size over the winter months. Then too, I never gained more than twelve pounds during the eight months of my pregnancy, so between the coat, which I was not required to take off in class if didn't want to, and loose clothing which was my habit to wear anyway, no one suspected I was pregnant.

The coat turned out to be a double blessing. Since I was terrified to leave my cat at home for fear of its being tortured, I made up my mind to take it with me everywhere I went. That meant school, too. I devised a sling out of one of my scarves which I wore under my coat and put the kitten in the sling. There she was carried on the long walks to and from school, and during school she sat quietly hidden under my coat. I always sat at the back of the classroom to draw as little attention to myself as possible and at lunch time I took Beebee into a restroom stall where I fed her with food I'd brought in my pocket. I've always believed that cat in her own way understood that she was being protected since she cooperated beautifully never making a peep at school, not even purring as was her habit whenever she sat in my lap at home. On the walk home from school she would poke her tiny head out of the top of my cape and mew or purr and enjoy the fresh air.

As time went on, my life with Phillip became increasingly impossible. The only real connection I had at the school was Mrs. Isenlore who was either a counselor or assistant principal, I can't remember which. For some reason she took an interest in me when I refused to take gym and called me into her office to inquire about the reason for my unwillingness to participate in that class. I remember her as a pretty woman, small and fine boned, with soft brown hair and a smile that warmed her eyes. I liked her at once. As I took a tentative seat across from her she didn't speak right away, but looked at me penetratingly though not harshly. I felt my face redden and I dropped my eyes and concentrated on my hands clasped in my lap. Almost without pause she asked me point blank if I were pregnant. There was no use in lying to her. I felt she could see right through me.

A fear swept over me. Now that it was known that I was pregnant, I wouldn't be allowed to come to school anymore. At this point it wasn't so much my education I was worried about losing; it was the only place I had to go besides my home which was no home. It was my only connection with normal people. It was the only place that made any sense at all.

She asked me a few more questions about my life and how it was that I ended up in Ann Arbor. The smallest interval of silence followed my answers to her questions although to me it felt like forever. Finally she answered in an upbeat and cheery voice "I think we can put you in a creative writing course to replace gym. Would you like that?"

I never wanted to hug anyone so much in my life as I did this woman who was going to help me keep my secret; who seemed to understand and want to help even though she hardly knew me. I was overwhelmed by her kindness and was barely able to get out of her office before the tears came. Relief flooded me at the knowledge that my one asylum would not be taken away. I walked home that afternoon with a light heart and Beebee safe in her sling under my coat!

Not quite two months into my stay in Ann Arbor, Phillip began beating me viciously whenever I did anything which displeased him which was often enough. I had as fine a collection of bruises as could be found anywhere on a dozen athletes. We still had to go back to Flint monthly for my visits to the obstetrician who would be delivering my baby and when my parents viewed with suppressed alarm the black and blue bruises on my arms and face they began asking questions. I lied stoutly, telling them I had tripped and fallen down the stairs. I don't think either one of them believed it especially in light of the fact they'd both been involved in domestic violence for many years, but during that time people were under the spell of *minding their own business* and of looking the other way. I told the same lie to my doctor who wasn't buying it that all of a sudden I was too clumsy to navigate the stairs and suggested counseling for my marriage. A bitter laugh escaped me at the thought of Phillip caring a rats' rear end whether our marriage did well or not, so I declined this help which even I knew would never work even if I'd wanted it to.

There were strong dual emotions concerning my plight; I desperately wanted someone to know what was happening to me and rescue me, and yet I didn't want anyone to know. On the one hand, I felt a lot of shame that I'd gotten myself into such a fix and that my marriage was a complete failure; on the other hand, fear that if I told anyone, I would be beaten even worse when we got back to Ann Arbor. So I held my piece for the time being.

Drugs were not as widespread when I was a teenager as they are now and I'd led a fairly sheltered life up until my marriage to Phillip. I'd never seen drugs so I didn't even know what they looked like or what behavioral changes they caused, nor had I ever known of anyone on drugs, or even had a conversation with my parents or anyone else about drugs but I didn't know how else to account for Phillip's possessed behavior. No one in their right mind would behave as he did. One evening he beat me so brutally that blood began to pour down my legs. I was terrified that the beating had brought on a miscarriage. Even Phillip became afraid and somewhat contrite when he saw me standing in a pool of blood clutching my stomach and crying and rushed me to the hospital.

They treated me and packed me full of some medication and sent me home and told me to stay in bed for a couple of days, no questions asked. It was a different world then and it seemed that people, even hospitals did not pry into people's personal lives for information about suspicious bruises or injuries. If you offered a lie as an excuse, it was quickly accepted. The universal attitude at that time was that if it didn't concern you, you didn't get involved in things that were none of your business. Thank God some things have changed and people, especially under aged children have recourse in such situations and are encouraged to speak up in the event of abuses, but at that time suffering in silence was preferred by victims, perpetrators, and those on the sidelines as well. I went home and tried to heal quietly taking care to stay out of Phillip's way and he also stayed away from me most of the time for the next few days. Maybe he felt shame and possibly some regret but apology was not his modus operandi.

I missed a lot of school during that period of time, calling in to Mrs. Isenlore that I was not feeling well. In a couple of days my bruises would be faded enough to cover with makeup, then I would return to school and pretend to be like everyone else.

But after I had recovered I found that nothing had changed. My next violent encounter came when he was in an arbitrary mood with a notion to hurt Beebee and I intervened. By now I was thoroughly worn out with his cruelty and my own anger was escalating to a level I knew I wouldn't be able to hide much longer which was scary. I was plagued with thoughts of killing him in his sleep and other unsavory methods of revenge or of running away never to be seen again. I was sure that one day soon coming he was going to start up with me and I was going to answer it with a violence of my own and perhaps get myself or the cat killed for my troubles. But at the moment somehow I was not going to allow him to hurt my cat again uncontested. He kicked the cat and I threw an alarm clock at him that caught him across the forehead and drew blood which sent him into an instant rage. He crossed the room in three strides and with his fist hit me in the face knocking me down. As blood poured from my nose, I screamed "Go to hell!!" At this point my anger if not my strength matched his and I was far too angry to care about the consequences which got me another punch in the face. I repeated my former instructions and got hit yet again. This went on until I was lying in a heap on the floor unable to move. He ranted around the apartment for a few more minutes and then left for the rest of the night. Beebee came as she always did after these episodes to sit and comfort me by washing my hands and battered face with her scratchy tongue.

The aloneness I'd learned to cope with all of my life expanded to such dimensions in this disastrous marriage that I'd been afraid of from the very beginning that I felt like all the hope had gone out of me. I was totally alone except for my unborn child and my kitten. It was them that I talked to about my thoughts and battered feelings, and it was God to Whom I poured out my lonely heart in those days. Of course, you feel alone when you are alone, but it is truly sad to feel alone when you are with someone who is supposed to care but doesn't.

Over the years I've seen more of this type two loneliness which I'd first witnessed in my own parent's marriage from the time I was a small child, but had hoped was only an exception and not the rule in human relations. I believe it to be the byproduct of self-centeredness and lack of communication. Whenever it's all about us there just is no room in our awareness to really see others and how we affect them or to really care if things are well with them or not, or if they have what they need from us to be happy. That's the difference between real love and the counterfeit emotions that pass for love but bear none of its fruit.

It seems to me that people ought to sit down when they speak of marriage and see if their definitions of love and commitment match. It's these differences in interpretation of what it means to love that are the major fault line in failing marriages. If you've said I love you to someone but feel it necessary to control them, or feel any sense of justice in punishing them for not reading your mind by means of verbal or physical abuse; to pop their bubble if they seem for the moment to be riding a little higher than you or to invalidate everything they say or feel, then you not only don't have the goods to be part of a successful marriage, but are altogether ignorant of the true character of love. I'll even go a step further to say that if these punishing tendencies are a part of your emotional makeup there's not even a decent chance that you could ever be happy on your own. Perhaps some effort to understand what love really means as described in the Bible in I Corinthians Chapter 13 would be a helpful place to start. We will all come short to varying degrees, but it's a good place to begin to understand the nature of love and what it takes to make a friendship or marriage work.

As for me, my life continued to be scenes from hell for another three months until we moved back to Flint in preparation for the birth of the baby. We stayed at my parents for a while since they were the ones who would help me after the baby was born while he was away at work and I continued school.

Phillips' abuses were now downsized to the verbal variety. I don't know that I can say it hurt any less only that I no longer had to offer bogus excuses for having a black eye or busted lip. I was greatly relieved that my little cat was no longer in danger, and I was far enough along in my pregnancy to not have to worry about a miscarriage brought on by violence.

Youth is miraculously resilient, and after the brutalities I had survived, the comparatively safe haven of my parents' home brought enough relief to make me look forward to the future. I continued school in Flint, taking only a two week break when Karl was born. I wasn't disappointed in my feelings about him. Having him was exactly the experience of love and belonging I had imagined it to be. Obviously, there were the frustrating parts for which no teenager is really emotionally equipped to deal with, but all in all it was a great experience. I must admit to my lack of wisdom as a first time parent. I was more a contemporary than a parent, but I adored him and took his natural infant's partiality for mother as evidence of his love for me.

During the last trimester of my pregnancy since I still couldn't go to a public school, Patsy's mother had arranged for me to attend a special school for pregnant teens so that I wouldn't get behind. I owed her as much thanks as anyone for helping me get my education during a difficult time. After Karl's birth I went back to Southwestern High School and graduated with my class which drew a huge sigh of relief from everyone including me. There were certainly many times over the past year and a half when I doubted seriously if I could ever get over the obstacles in the path of my education.

We stayed with my parents until shortly after my graduation. Karl was about a year old when we moved into a nearby neighborhood apartment complex. As soon as I was no longer under the protection of my parents, Phillip instantly returned to his old ways; demeaning me verbally and occasionally hitting me…only now, there was a frightening new development in his life; heroin.

With the advent of Phillips' use of this hideous drug came the revolving cycle of domestic violence, violent crimes, court, jail, and rehab. I was completely naïve about drugs of any kind and hadn't the slightest idea of the horrific mess someone could make of their life nor of the ongoing drama for those who were a part of their lives. Even hearing about it is a distant second to actually being an inside witness to this tragedy. I won't go into the myriad incidences of everyday living with someone addicted to heroin; just that life was an ongoing drama of violence perpetrated against me and/or perfect strangers; of the frantic and unreasonable moods and demands of the user; the police at the door at any hour of the day or night; coming home from work to find other junkies lying around your house in a stupor; court dates; jail visitation; and attending the court required counseling sessions in rehab. And last, but certainly not least, his repeated return to the drug.

This looking into the face of someone known and not being able to find them because a stranger now controls their mind and actions making them capable of things you never dreamed they'd be able to do was not something you could ever get used to. The dark cloud of this existence that hangs continuously over the user and anyone connected with his life is that nothing can be enjoyed even that is good. It's living with the knowledge that if continued, there absolutely will be tragedy. You just don't know the date yet.

At this time you might be asking yourself why I stayed. I asked myself that question a million times. But simply put, to me divorce was a thing to be devoutly avoided. Throughout his addiction we were separated more often than not anyway by work, which oddly he never missed, his street life, and various jail sentences ninety days or under, and rehab. There finally did come a time when for Karl's and my safety it was necessary to separate from him which I did, but we never divorced. My father had taken me to a lawyer friend of our family's after having a talk with me about divorcing Phillip. I didn't have to be convinced of the logic of getting clear of this disastrous marriage that was greatly disturbing my health, my piece of mind, and my very safety and that of my son's and so I consented to an appointment with the lawyer, Attorney Fred Robinson. I felt pretty resolute but when it came to actually signing the paper, I crumpled up and wept. All of a sudden, justified though it was it just felt so wrong. Even I don't know what happened in that moment, only somewhere along the way my terror of him died and was replaced by pity and a sorrowful understanding that it wasn't really me he was hitting in his tirades; it was whatever was responsible for his fear and unhappiness. In the end, I couldn't stay for it, but I no longer hated him.

During the rehab and counseling times which I attended with Phillip, I met many other recovering drug addicts and heard their troubled stories in group therapy. Over and over again my solitude was opened and invaded by the knowledge and close contact of other realities as harsh as or worse than my own had been. I remember cherishing the solitude I'd known all my life compared to things I heard in group therapy. At least my solitude had been furnished with beautiful things even though I had no one to share those things with, but for junkies the only beauty was the needle and what it brought. All were running away from a reality that was too heavy to carry—many with memories of childhood which were gruesome indeed. Some kids survive, some don't, but too many times the survivors have had to find a way to endure. Sometimes drugs and alcohol are the chosen anodynes for survival.

As time went on I understood much better how devastating this drug really was and how precious few there were who completely recovered. Many retraced those recovered footsteps back to the source of their relief. For them life could not be faced without drugs. In fact, I only ever met one person who got clean and stayed clean. Through those years in frustration and disbelief the neighborhood attended a lot of funerals of young, black men dead from the street life. Without being melodramatic in the least, it was soul sickening to witness this incredible waste of human life and potential!

The main issue for a recovering junkie is being continually vulnerable to contact with those he used to get high with who are not in rehab. Drug cronies came by with regularity to lure Phillip back into the old life. It's not that unusual for ordinary frustrations to overwhelm a junkie to the point that makes the offer irresistible, and Phillip was never able to resist for very long. It was my contention that if you were in this kind of trouble, the only way out was to move to another city where no one knew you or what you had been; where you could start over. There was also considerable pressure on me to whom the methadone pills (withdrawal medication) were entrusted. Sometimes he would corner me and viciously demand more than the allowed dosage, or search until he found my various hiding places and then take what he wanted.

During the time he was in over his head he was using approximately $800.00 a day in heroin and cocaine. Shooting up *speedballs*; a cocktail of both drugs combined was his preferred method of destruction. He'd always been an industrious person and was the youngest black journeyman electrician in the state of Michigan working for his fathers' company. He'd always made excellent money and loved expensive clothes, furniture, or whatever. And even while he was deep into drugs, he still went faithfully to work every day which isn't exactly stereotypical behavior for someone on heroin. But even though he made really good money, it wasn't enough to cover household expenses and an $800.00 a day habit; hence the drug related crimes began. Sometimes he would drive out of state to steal reels of electrical wiring or whatever he could find from the jobsites of other competitive electrical companies which he could sell, but most often his crimes were closer to home. Once over a dispute with someone else in the drug world, he did a drive by shooting. Luckily the man was not killed. On the heels of that crime, he held up a woman who was the proprietor of a small restaurant at gunpoint. For these two crimes, his lawyer informed him that he could get up to fifteen years in prison. The details of this period of time are still hazy to me. Phillip's father was the one who dealt with all the legalities of his situation. I only remember the salient features of the nightmare.

The trial was postponed repeatedly during which time he had Phillip admitted to a very prestigious drug rehabilitation center in Lexington, Kentucky where he spent nine months. I suppose this action was taken in the hopes that becoming drug free would perhaps produce a more favorable outcome in court. Before being admitted into the rehab center, he was approached by the narcotic squad with the proposal of a significant reduction in his jail sentence in return for his cooperation in helping them bust some drug houses he'd been frequenting over the years. When he mentioned this plan to me, I instantly had bad feelings about it. Fifteen years of your life gone is certainly no light thing and the chance to reduce it naturally tempting, but snitching seemed like a death sentence to me and therefore not a good trade since you'd be looking over your shoulder for the rest of your life. I understand the need for the law to pursue those that trade in this devastating market, yet at the same time it seems a blatant disregard for the lives of those trying to recover from drugs and that of their families. In the criminal world, you snitch; you die…sooner or later. But he decided to comply and take his chances. I never actually knew all that this entailed other than that his body was wired and he went to drug houses to buy drugs.

He was understandably extremely paranoid during this time. He wouldn't sit in front of a window or walk out of the front door first. Once in real anxiety he pushed me out of the door before he would walk out. A deep depression overtook him when the reality of his decision became crystal clear after being poisoned with strychnine. He'd gone to the pool hall for a few games and remembered leaving his drink on a table and going to the men's room. He came out, quickly finished his beer, and left. The pool hall was very near where we lived and by the time he got home he was vomiting profusely and completely unable to stand up for the pain in his body. I called an ambulance which arrived very shortly and we were soon at the hospital where his stomach was pumped, the contents revealing the strychnine. Unfortunately, his choice was irrevocable and the terrifying feeling that his days were numbered came over him.

We separated not long after the poisoning. Karl spent part of his day at nursery school and stayed with grandma and grandpa while I worked, and the rest of the time he was with me. The realization that the people Phillip had crossed would stop at nothing to get back at him was one that I lived with hourly. My nerves were completely undone. I had no idea whether Karl or I would be targets as a part of their revenge, but I felt that the only sane decision was to remove us as far from the storm center as possible. My word had carried no weight in this impossible marriage and I'd had no influence to change the course of events. Phillip had been drawn to this lifestyle, had followed its destructive path to a place I could no longer even bear to witness.

After his return from Lexington, Kentucky, he seemed a different person—nothing like the wild, angry man I'd known; more sober, his usual swagger quite gone, and there was a determined air about him to begin his life again and to leave his ruined past behind. He was quite a stranger to me and I marveled that I'd ever shared a life with him at all or that he was my son's father. I mechanically talked over with him the conditions under which he might visit with Karl; I wanted no more drama for him. He agreed without contention to everything I said. We talked about a few other non-essentials, mostly small talk and then he was gone. Life went on in this calm way for a short period of time; I have no memory now whether it was one month or six.

The first calm I'd ever seen in the drama of Phillip's life was not to last. Shortly after I'd gotten in from work one evening, the phone rang. It was Phillip's step-mother calling to tell me he'd been shot and was in the hospital in critical condition. He'd been in the car with a young woman when two men came up on each side of the car. The woman was shot three times, and he was shot six times at point blank range. The gunmen fled, and miraculously Phillip got out of the car and ran a short distance to the nearest house, knocking on someone's door and asking if they would call an ambulance.

My first sight of him when I walked into the hospital room nearly caused me to faint. He was hooked up to many machines and his intestines were in a bag at his side. I was told by the doctors that he might not make it. Struggling for composure, I walked over to the bed. He was fully conscious and looked up at me. I said that I'd already told Karl that his father would be alright as if the promise would make it so. He smiled and said he *would* be alright, and I tried to believe him. I was overwhelmed with sadness at the inescapable end of drugs and crime…the waste was nauseating.

One of the many negatives of heroin use is that even after you've been off it for a while, your blood doesn't clot properly and he hadn't been clean for very long. As the days went by, his condition worsened and he developed peritonitis. Just before they did a tracheotomy, while he could still speak, he told me who it was that had shot him. My first response was to give those names to the police as soon as I left the hospital. But on second thought, I made a swift decision that I would never tell anyone who did it. First of all, if they did this to Phillip, nothing would stop them from targeting Karl or myself. Secondly, I knew that no one lives this life for long without it catching up to them. I would leave them to the fate of their chosen lives and to the judgment of God. Whether I was right or wrong, I've never regretted that decision.

There really are not many conclusions for those in the drug world; either jail, over dosing, or death by violence, and I had faith that if they did not change their lives, one or the other would catch up to them soon enough without me placing myself and my child in danger. They came into my place of work a couple of times following the shooting and though I was sick with fear, I pretended not to be and took no special notice of them. Eventually, when the police never came after them, they must have concluded that Phillip never said anything to me, or that I never said anything to the police, and so they left me alone. And I'd like to jump ahead a little to say that sure enough, less than two years later I heard about their deaths from over dose. There are no happy endings in the world of drugs and crime.

Phillip never spoke again after he disclosed the gunmen's' names, but went downhill swiftly. He bled constantly from his nose and mouth so that it was impossible for the nursing staff even to keep him cleaned up. I can never explain the alternating feelings of impotent rage and broken sorrow that overwhelmed me as I helplessly watched the unnecessary, approaching death of so young a person. Here he lay dying without ever having won his father's approval which he'd needed so desperately; without a wife's love or even loving, longtime friends at his bedside. These realities just seemed brutally tragic along with the fact that he had not found anything meaningful enough in this life to turn him aside from the fate that was now claiming him. Almost three weeks to the date after the shooting he was dead.

Though I can't say I was surprised at his death, I was blanched by shock. The aftermath of this part of my life left me on the verge of a nervous breakdown. Suddenly, I was responsible for an enormous amount of debt. Phillips' death left me stunned and unable to make decisions or move forward for a time. I felt beached in a cold and frightening new world that I was sorely unprepared for and was completely at a loss as to how or where to begin. Emotionally I was numb and foundering.

Shattered though I was, I could still feel an invisible force holding me together. The Chinese have a saying, "The journey of a thousand miles begins with the first step." There was no bridge to the past…and so, without knowing where I was going, with only my blind faith, I stepped out on the road of my life and just started to walk.

Chapter 2

# A Closer Look at the Village that Raised the Child

Earl C.
Eleanor C.
Esther Jones
J.W. Clark
Mildred
Patsy
Mrs. Booker
Vivian Tripp Wheeland
Bro. Wilson
Karen

# Preceding Remarks

In all fairness to the people you will read about in the following mini-bio's, it should be remembered that while my early judgments have been seasoned with the vantage point of time, when originally processed they were the one dimensional perceptions and memories of a very young child up through late teen years. I have delivered the experiences as they appeared to me then and what were their effects on me for the sake of setting forth the foundations on which my solitude was constructed.

In order to tell my story, obviously something must be said of those whose lives were intermingled with mine and the effects they had on me for good or evil, but is by no means a complete slide of any one individual. My perceptions of these people were in relationship only to myself. Obviously, there were other areas of their lives and accomplishments to which I was completely oblivious.

An excellent example of the evolution of my early perceptions became apparent to me with the meeting of my birth mother. After a few years of processing the unavoidable experiences with which life teaches us, both my own and also in witnessing the trials of others, I found that time had ripened my judgments and given me both the ability to see the big picture more clearly, and even more importantly to be able to imagine myself in someone else's reality.

Since I was adopted, there was the usual era of unawareness of my birth mother. When I finally became old enough that there was a reasonable chance I was going to hear it around town or at school my adoptive mother decided it was time to tell me about Shirley. I then passed from unawareness to curiosity which flickered on and off for many years, not yet strong enough to produce the spark that would eventually spur me to actively searching her out. In the meantime, there was a lot of unspoken angst between my adoptive mother and me. Our spirits contended continually. I felt alarm, puzzlement, and guilt at not being able to love her. And I knew beyond a shadow of a doubt that she not only didn't really like me, but also had an active contempt for me…but why? Years of emotional confusion transpired before the answers came.

Through the years, there were instances when something was said about Shirley in relationship to me that while I wasn't able to unravel the source of their ire, I understood without being told that my adoptive parents, particularly my mother, disliked Shirley intensely. But the question lingered…why? Our relationship was not close enough to encourage me to ask personal questions. Times were different then; the line of delineation between adults and children was much deeper. Children were not free to question adults the way they are invited to do now especially not on such sensitive topics that even they may not have come to a full understanding of.

When I finally met Shirley, I was nearly twenty-two years old. In just a few short visits the answer to the riddle between me, her, and my adoptive mother came clearly into focus. I remember laughing insanely one night over the irony or the whole thing.

A lonely, childless woman (Eleanor) in a dead marriage feels she needs a child to give her life meaning although she despises the woman (Shirley) through whom the opportunity of a child is coming. The child however, is a miniature of her birth parent, and so is a continual thorn in the side of that woman (Eleanor). The child doesn't even know of her birth mother's existence let alone her personal characteristics and wonders why numerous harmless things about her seem to agitate her mother (Eleanor), and to compound the existing problem everything that the birth mother hated about that woman, the child also hated without understanding why.

It seems that genetics had a healthy share in playing devil's advocate. How it must have goaded my adoptive mother disliking Shirley as she did, to have to look into Shirley's face every day that she was raising me. Unbeknownst to me, I had so many of the physical and mental characteristics of Shirley which she hated, such as smelling everything and generally being an intense and private person. Seeing how ironic the whole thing was left me feeling disconcerted and extremely sad. My judgments of my adoptive mother softened with the understanding.

Though I would never quite feel the maternal connection with her that we both needed, I at least would never dislike her anymore. I learned to feel truly sorry for the way her life had turned out. Each of us in our own way was disappointed of valid and urgent needs we'd had, and grappled, not always successfully, in the void. I don't believe originally that there was any planned malice involved. It was just one of billions of human plans that just didn't turn out as expected.

Likewise with Shirley, after our original meeting, I hung around quite a bit asking my questions. So unawareness changed into curiosity and then into knowledge. My initial acquaintance with Shirley ignited anger. Shirley had five other children. She'd kept the boys and given away the two girls, myself and a sister. For this I was angry. And also, for the fact that only one of my four brothers was faring well with her as a single parent. I felt she was extremely remiss in her duty to her children. It was not until I'd come into the knowledge of her youth and her losses that my opinions again softened.

As a young girl, Shirley had been the only child of her doting mother and father. When Shirley was nine years old, her mother died suddenly of a congenital heart disease and her father gave over his care of her to relatives who viewed her only in the light of a nuisance and a domestic servant. She essentially lost both parents at once and went from being petted and loved to being unwanted for the duration of her childhood in which she endured not only physical, but spirit destroying emotional deprivation that would shape the rest of her life.

What great needs overtook her spirit in that harsh, unloving environment? Because of my own solitude I knew the answers to that question. In an instant, I forgave her for whatever hurts I may have suffered from decisions she made in her wilderness.

When I considered the very real needs and fears that drove my adoptive mother and my birth mother, and the capacity life often has of being able to turn us into people we never meant to become, it made it much easier to forgive them their failures. Besides, whatever failures existed in these women and however it affected me is only one slide of them and in no way a complete representation of the whole individual.

Wisdom dictates that there are many unseen and unknown variables in every life. Until all the facts are in and every motive perfectly understood (which is never possible for mere mortals) we put ourselves through unnecessary emotional and spiritual turmoil nurturing negative feelings concerning people who are struggling with this life the same as we are. If someone is hurting us to the extent we are being personally damaged, it may become necessary for us to distance ourselves from them whether friend or family member. Still, we must protect our minds and solitudes from being cluttered with negativity and unforgiveness by being merciful in our judgments. So, as you read the accounts I experienced with the people who made up my world, remember they are isolated accounts of my own connection with these people and by no means an absolute judgment on anyone's entire character.

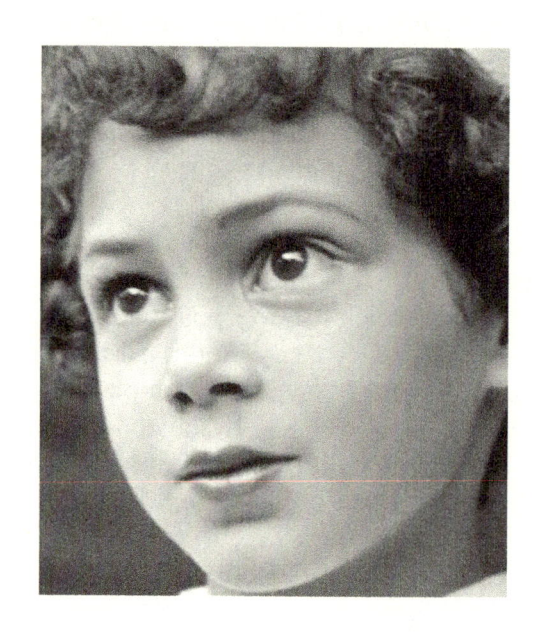

The child

## Earl C.

My adoptive father had a rough persona and Harlem candor that raised a lot of eyebrows and fists almost to his dying day. He never held back telling people exactly what he thought emphatically and often at the top of his lungs. He had a great sense of humor and in later years an uncanny resemblance both physically and in personality, even down to speech and voice inflection as, Redd Foxx, the famous comedian.

Like many men of his generation he wasn't especially comfortable wading into topics of any deep emotional import, and even at a young age I could sense where those boundaries were. There weren't hugs and kisses, and "I love you's" from him. He just wasn't the warm fuzzy sort. Then too, I'd found out before I was very old from my adoptive mother that he hadn't been knocked out about adopting a child from the very beginning. Aside from this, he was good natured and generally kind to me.

In many ways he was an enigma. Once in a great while I would get glimpses of what really mattered to him or of things that had hurt him from the past, but it was mostly things spoken of in the heat of a moment and in passing rather than anything expounded on during a one on one conversation. Usually it was political issues or racial injustices that drew the deepest responses from him. I'd never seen him lose his composure until the deaths of Medgar Evers, John and Robert Kennedy, and Martin Luther King. He wept uncontrollably for days at their untimely and senseless deaths.

The soft spots in his character surfaced whenever the ice cream boy came through the neighborhood. Us kids could hear the bells on that ice cream cart ringing several blocks away giving us plenty of time to go in and torment a parent for the necessary funds. But there were always kids who didn't have money. Then you would find Earl C. in a circle of kids passing out dimes like it was Christmastime. He couldn't stand to see anyone left out, especially when it came to eating. He was an extremely generous man when it came to money, possessions, or lending a hand in community matters.

He was never mean, unless he'd been drinking, and then fear was not only highly appropriate, but compulsory. If there was any bright spot at all to be found in his drinking, it was that he was a periodic drinker rather than a continual alcoholic. At our house, supper was promptly at 5:30pm, and if Earl C. was not in attendance, he was drinking, and we knew what was coming. We would spend a tense evening waiting, pretending not to be aware of what his absence portended; going to bed knowing there would be no sleep, nerves knotted. I used to wish fervently that I could just disappear while listening for his car to pull into the driveway in the early a.m. hours. Almost from the second he stumbled through the door, he was screaming, cussing mad. Down the hallway he would come, flinging open our bedroom doors where we lay afraid even to move, hoping that the silence would cause him to go away, but he always demanded that we get up. Then we were herded like sheep to the kitchen where we would spend the next few hours listening to him ranting about the duplicity of those he dealt with in his work. His shouts were accentuated by fist-pounding on the kitchen table so violent that even the salt and pepper shakers jumped.

Bewilderment, shame, and anger accompanied my fear. Bewilderment as to why he asked questions to which neither a yes, nor no would do; though silence only served to refuel his tirade; and vicious, scarring pronouncements against our characters, and the physical violence to which he sometimes resorted; shame, because I knew the neighbors could hear; and anger because I couldn't for the life of me understand why my mother knowing hours in advance what was coming, would not just get in the car and not be there for it. I would much have preferred spending the night in the car than ever being around Earl C. when he was drunk. Once in particular, when I was about nine years old, I could see his swaying silhouette in the doorway of my bedroom, and smell the liquor that permeated his presence. He was silent for just a moment. Fear overcame me to the point that I shook uncontrollably causing the headboard on the bed to bang the wall. Finally he spoke with pure contempt the words "You're a breeder just like your mother." I did not know exactly what those words meant, but I knew it wasn't anything good.

For at least two weeks after one of these episodes, black clouds of gloom, resentment and chilling silence would hang over our home until the daily routine blurred the memory of it. I both loved and hated the coming of Christmas. I loved it for its' wonderful festive self, and hated it because I knew beyond a doubt that sometime during the holiday Earl C. would get drunk and ruin it.

Only a couple of times in my life did I take it on myself to confront him about his explosive behavior while drinking. Once, when I was ten after we had endured a particularly brutal evening with him, I got up the next morning frightened but determined to ask him why he'd said such awful things about us and why he hit mother. I knocked on his bedroom door, my knees knocking together and my throat parched with fear. When it opened, the sight of him nearly destroyed my nerve, but I had to do something, so I told him the awful things he'd said to us the night before and asked him why he had hit my mother. He was purely astonished and looked at me as though I had two heads both void of sense and indignantly said he would never in his life say or do such things, and even if he had, he wouldn't have meant them. Young as I was, I never believed him. In my mind you couldn't say those hateful things unless somewhere deep in your heart you'd thought them first. I felt sure that drinking just revealed what was there all along.

The second time I resisted Earl C. about his drinking was on New Year's Day when I was thirteen years old and therefore invincible. I knew since he hadn't come home that night that he was out drinking and was going to come in showing out, but instead of the usual fear, a consuming rage built up in me over that long night. I was sick to death of his unreasonable behavior, and the way every holiday was ruined because of it. True to his habits, he came in shouting. I could literally feel my fuse burning down to the powder; then he hit my mother. My anger broke instantly. We were in the kitchen fixing something to eat when he'd come in, so there were cooking utensils on the counter. I didn't even look; I just grabbed the one nearest me and whacked him across the head as hard as I could, yelling in unalloyed rage "If you ever hit my mother again, I will kill you!"

I never saw anyone sober up so fast. Everything came to an immediate halt. Our eyes were locked; mine blazing with hatred, his stunned, bloodshot, and unbelieving, and my mother holding her breath probably waiting for me to be knocked to the floor. After an intense silent moment of eyes locked which seemed interminable, he spoke softly, almost as if to himself, "If I'd have ever talked to my father that way, he would've killed me." I did not answer, nor was I sorry. With the intensity of my anger still intact, we all stood stock still for an indeterminate amount of time; probably half a minute, then he just turned, coat still on, and walked out the door. We heard his car start up and then he was gone. My spirit expanded with the confrontation. I would never again be paralyzed by fear of him when he was drinking. We didn't see him for several days but the good that came of it was that though I'm sure he still drank occasionally, he never came home drunk again and that was just fine with me.

Earl C. was very much a man of his people and was not one to sit on the sidelines watching the battle during the Civil Rights movement; he was in the big, fat, middle of it. He marched with Martin Luther King, and participated in events with Medgar Evers. He was also quite a follower of Malcolm X, reading anything connected with his ministry and also closely followed the accomplishments of the black community in buying and thoroughly reading every Jet Magazine ever printed. Growing up, some of his passions and loyalties were confusing to me since Martin Luther King and Malcolm X were at opposite poles concerning their views on segregation, violence, and opinions of white people and how they were to figure into the final solution of racism though it's probably a more realistic statement to say that many black people during those turbulent times were able to relate to the strategies of both leaders.

Loving politics kept my father involved in all local and statewide elections. In those days, an approaching election season filled those of us who could not escape being drafted into his service with dread. The services of my best friend Patsy and I were commandeered for weeks at a time for the passing out tracts for whatever Democrat was running for whatever position; John Kennedy, John Reigle, Dale Kildee, and our first black mayor Floyd Mcree to name a few. Election Day was not for the faint of heart in our household. Nonparticipation was not an option, nor was any consideration of a Republican candidate which for Earl C. was anathema. Eating on the go, standing in the rain, wind, and cold or whatever dreary November weather became our lot at the polls; passing out tracts and more tracts in the hopes that some poor soul had come undecided as to how they would vote. Imagine that!! And when the polls closed, passing out on a couple of folding chairs pulled together, or in whatever unoccupied corner we could find while the election results came in after which we could finally go home in exhaustion and relief. By that time, I didn't care who won the election. It is the *quality* time I most remember spending with Earl C.

Several lasting imprints he left on me were, 1.) Never ask anybody for anything; And 2.) Never speak about your family business to anyone or betray a family member. You stay in their corner even if last night you tried to kill each other. 3.) Never tell anybody anything you don't have to. I loused this one up more than has been good for me, but then I did learn a lot from those mistakes, and 4.) He was also not less than obsessive concerning manners, especially table manners. A breach of etiquette such as using fingers to push food onto a fork, or spooning your soup in the wrong direction would earn you a bruising rap on the knuckles with his dinner knife. The wasting of food to a man who had survived Harlem and the depression was a fearful sin that was guaranteed to bring on a lengthy furious sermon on the evils of having eyes-bigger-than-your-belly.

Most breaches of manners were extremely offensive to him and usually were unpleasantly remarked upon to the shame of the offender. I remember that once a young man knocked on our door to ask directions. My father opened the door and when that fellow stepped into the house, and made the unfortunate mistake of not removing his hat in the presence of women, he was grabbed by the collar and the belt of his trousers and heaved out the door. I thought that response was a little over the top and wondered if something more had transpired than what I saw, but on second thought I knew my father was perfectly capable of being incensed over a hat not removed.

Earl C. loved the pleasures of the table possibly more than anyone I ever saw. Meals were accentuated with moans of pure enjoyment. There wasn't usually much conversation at the table until after his appetite was sated. After supper and a small nap, the evening was a veritable holiday every night of the week. He loved watching TV until it went off the air. (Yes folks, back then it actually did go off the air usually not later than 2:00am) As long as it was on, that's where he would be, eating and cussing out the bad guys. If you ventured from your room after TV went off the air you would find him snoring contentedly in his favorite chair in front of a fuzzy whistling screen.

Each program was accompanied by a small entrée of its own. He enjoyed tearing the kitchen apart making *treats*. Gumbo made out of Campbell's soup, with a can of shrimp or crab meat added; bratwurst and cheese and crackers; and a double-chocolate malt. Even someone like me who adored chocolate could only take one rich sip. It was made from chocolate milk, chocolate ice cream, chocolate malt, and Hershey's chocolate syrup which to me was the sickest of all his concoctions. My mother usually disappeared for the night after supper because of the party atmosphere that took over the family room and kitchen. I completely understood and also spent most all my evenings in my bedroom in my own little world. So, it was Earl C. and the dog (who hung around for the treats that were surely coming his way) all night long in front of the T.V., and he seemed perfectly happy with that arrangement.

# Eleanor C.

Eleanor C., my adoptive mother, was quietly tucked away in what was left of herself after a lifetime of ill health, an empty interracial marriage, and the multiple frustrations that made up her life. She didn't speak much about her thoughts and feelings or of her past before she married Earl C. She was a very industrious person always with some project on hand whether it was housework, the ceramics that she loved, her flower garden, or the dogs she bred and sold. For a number of years she was a hairdresser with her own beauty salon but that too was plagued by racism. As soon as one of her white clients found out she was married to a black man, her business immediately fell off and she'd have to start again. She pursued these interests with an energy that was hard to fathom.

Eleanor C. was a frail woman whose eyes suggested sorrow and resolve without a hint of happiness. She'd always been in poor health even as a child and had undergone thirty-one surgeries in her life, most of which were major, but she always rallied quickly if not fully and as soon as she could stand on her feet, she was back to work. She was neither a quitter, nor a complainer. While I was growing up she was always battling one illness or another; in and out of doctors' offices and hospitals. To my knowledge my father rarely visited her when she was in hospital and seemed to think her illnesses not quite credible. In spite of, or because of, I never knew which, she persevered in trials. She was without a doubt one of the steeliest individuals I'd ever seen.

When I came on the scene, she transferred a lot of that drive to me. I was put through better than a decade of ballet, tap, and jazz dance lessons, violin lessons, singing lessons, baton twirling lessons, modeling lessons; piano lessons all which she usually attended. Often her presence at these lessons made me uncomfortable. I was always acutely conscious of the intensity of her focus on me to the point I would sometimes catch her mouthing the words of songs I was singing for my voice instructor.

It had the effect of being both extremely comical and insanely obsessed to me. Even I was aware of the fact that I was on an assembly line to become someone she could vicariously live through, and I felt by some intuition that it was a far more important goal for her than it was for me, though it was not a concern I felt I could speak up about. She might possibly have achieved her intentions had she let me attend classes alone. Her presence was particularly aggravating to me. It made me extremely self-conscious as none of the other children's parents ever stuck around more than a few minutes if at all and it always divided my concentration. More often than not I was trying desperately to stifle a giggle or hide the frustration of not wanting to attempt things for the first time in front of her, and of generally just wanting the experience to be between me, the instructor, and the class if there was one. But she felt a need to be there and so took her solace regardless of the long term consequences.

Eleanor C. had suffered three miscarriages and undergone a hysterectomy by her late forties and so was childless when I came along. Very early on I understood by some strange osmosis that a lot was riding on me concerning her and I felt this subtle obligation throughout my childhood and well into my teens. I believe I was to some extent an investment in her future.

She was ingenious when it came to mapping out ways to get what she wanted. You don't have to be brilliantly imaginative to grasp the motives behind the deeds of a frustrated and lonely woman. Though being the object of those plans was both annoying and uncomfortable, I don't blame her anymore, but at the time it was still quite something to behold her strategies. She wasn't to my thinking always scrupulous in the methods she employed to achieve her goals but most of the time she ended up somewhere in the neighborhood of her plans.

One particular time still stands out in my memory and somewhat epitomizes the kinds of subtle manipulation I both witnessed and felt the effects of frequently. When I was fifteen, my voice instructor, Vivian Wheeland, entered me in a very prestigious national singing contest at Bloomington Indiana Music Conservatory. The competition was for students between ages seventeen to thirty-five, and I was only fifteen so, I was on fire with excitement to think they'd thought I was good enough to compete in a national event designed for older, more experienced students. For me it was more a miraculous opportunity to get to see and hear great singers from all over the country!

I had worked for nearly a year with Mrs. Wheeland on the three selections we'd chosen for the competition and after I had performed them and was judged I was totally ecstatic to find that I had scored so well that if there'd been such a thing as fourth place, I would have won it! I'd never expected to do so well among so many gifted vocalists and felt sure with this fresh inspiration that in time I would do even better. And as if that wasn't enough, I'd been invited by the head of the conservatory, Mr. Appleman, to accompany him and his wife to the complimentary opera that was performed by the students of Bloomfield Conservatory for the contestants. I felt like I'd died and gone to Heaven!

But the night before we were to head back home while packing our bags, my mother took me aside and told me that when we got home and people asked about how the competition had gone, I was to tell them that I had taken third place. All the fine glow of this amazing event instantly began to drain out of my heart. I didn't want to lie! Why should I have to? What was wrong with the success that I had truly achieved? Had I not done well enough being the youngest contender, permitted to participate in the event because it was agreed that I had a talent worth bending the rules for? Wasn't it enough that I had scored high enough to be just under third place among so many gifted vocalists from all over the country? My mother would tell everyone that I had won third place. How could I expose her for a liar by giving a different account of the competition? I chose never to speak of it rather than lie which stole my opportunity to share it with anyone. My satisfaction in that success evaporated with the understanding that for my mother it wasn't good enough. This was one of many events when her ambitions widened the gulf between us.

Though our oil and water natures never would mix my views of my adoptive mother softened considerably with age. I was in my late teens before I knew anything about her life prior to her marriage to my adoptive father. On the whole she'd had a pretty rough life and it wasn't hard to imagine how she had become so manipulative.

As a child her mother had preferred her brother William to her. It was my understanding that Eleanor's father had been especially cruel and Eleanor reminded her mother of him, consequently, their relationship was not a close one. She'd also been married once before Earl C. to a man who idolized his mother so much that Eleanor could never quite measure up which eventually ended the marriage. The knowledge of her unfortunate past did nothing to mend our relationship but it extinguished the flame of my anger toward her which was no small miracle. My inability either to love or forgive her had been confusing and the cause of much guilt during my childhood and youth. At one juncture of my life, I didn't care if I ever saw her again, but God helped me to forgive her for the harm she did me, and when she died at the age of eighty-four I was immensely thankful that there was no more anger in my heart toward her.

# Esther Jones

My grandmother was five feet tall and possibly about ninety pounds of pure austerity. She didn't talk a lot, nor was she big on physical demonstrations of affection, but she had ways of making you know you were loved.

Esther Jones was the first person I ever truly loved and admired, and the more I witnessed her loyalty and sense of justice, the more I idolized her. She was born in England on April 13, 1989, along with a twin sister. I'm not certain just when it was that she came to the United States, but I was told she married in this country and had two children, a son named William, and my adoptive mother Eleanor C. It was hard to imagine them being related for they were worlds apart in their thinking. My grandmother's relationship to her daughter seemed awkward at times. There was something between them that had somehow been patched up, but felt more like determination than love. My grandmother being fiercely loyal wouldn't have permitted anything to separate her from anyone she loved, but there's no doubt she paid a price at the hands of indignant relatives for refusing to turn her back on her daughter who had widely crossed the line in marrying a black man and adopting a half-breed child.

My child's memory retains her as nearly perfect, but it wasn't until I was in my twenties that I came to appreciate the breadth and depth of her quiet integrity. I was pretty young, eight or nine, when a chance presented itself for me to witness her integrity in the stoic stand she took against indignant relatives during an unfortunate confrontation regarding my being unwelcome in their homes. The family had drawn a clean line in the sand between themselves and the offender; she chose to side with her daughter and me which put the rest of the family's collective nose out of joint. Though they reluctantly conceded their right to cast us out because of repercussions at her hands, in their hearts they were divided against her which grief was irremediable. When she spoke on this issue which was brief and ever to the point, family members swallowed their ire with none too good grace for the sake of future remunerations which years later I understood to be her Last Will and Testament, and so the family received me, not for my sake, but for hers.

In hindsight, I'm awed by the magnitude of her sense of justice. In the first place, technically, I wasn't even really her blood kin. Secondly, I understood that she was fully aware that her edict didn't change her family's thinking concerning me one bit, but she would not allow anyone to offend or openly reject me. In the end their desire to remain in Esther's good graces was enough to deter them from their natural inclination to snub me. But even though I was allowed in their homes now, I had no interest in associating with people I knew despised me, but for reasons that were not clear to me my grandmother insisted that I take my place at their tables. Thankfully the occasions were few and of short duration.

I'm sure she originally opposed Eleanor's marriage, but once it was done, that was it. She never reproached her thereafter even though the rest of the family including Eleanor's own brother with whom she had been quite close completely disowned her. Whatever her personal views on mixed-marriage were, she put them in storage. I once heard her say "Love goes where it's sent, even if it's to a pigpen." This statement was by no means a slur cast on my dad, only that she gave love a wide berth and blamed no one for their heart's choice. It was a rather romantic notion for someone which such a phlegmatic nature as hers.

She got along very well with Earl C. when she came to visit us. There seemed to be no strain between them though I noticed that she was always more talkative with him than with anyone else. Her very keen, but wry sense of humor mingled with his more brusque sense of comedy was really very entertaining at the dinner table.

One of my favorite memories of her was that once when my mother was at work, grandma had to take me to the dentist and I was so mortally afraid of dentists that the knowledge of an appointment was kept from me right up until we pulled into the parking lot. Such was the case when grandmother took me, and as soon as we pulled into the dentist's parking lot, big tears began to run down my face. Though my grandmother was a stern woman, she couldn't stand to see me crying in terror. When we got into the waiting room, which next to having my name called, was the worst part, it was so crowded with people that I wasn't even granted the small comfort of sitting beside her.

It was a dimly lit, dreary waiting room, and the only interesting thing in it was a well-kept aquarium full of exotic, brightly colored fish. The only two seats available were at opposite ends of the room, so I sat down next to the aquarium, and grandma sat across the room. The room was a menagerie of magazines and newspapers; not a face could be seen. I sat alternately looking into the aquarium and then to my grandmother who watched with concern as I worried myself to death about the atrocities that were about to happen to me. Once though, while the solid wall of newspapers and magazines around the room was unbroken, I glanced up at my grandmother and an unexpected burst of laughter escaped me, for as soon as I'd looked up, my grandmother had stealthily stuck out and then quickly retracted her bottom false teeth to divert me from my fears. It must have been supposed by the denizens of that waiting room that I'd had a momentary fit of hysteria, because when they peered over their reading material to see what was so funny, my grandmother was looking innocently into her lap and the rest of the room was as dreary as it ever was without any reason at all for mirth. But I knew in my heart that nothing short of love could have caused such a breach of decorum in her behavior. True, it was short lived, but I'd had a small reprieve from my terrors.

Grandma died September 16, 1965 when I was only fourteen, and I miss her very much even after all these years, but she'd left the unforgettable memory of her love that is a huge part of the foundation of my life for which I'm deeply grateful. Whenever there's a bit of trouble in my life I can still feel the quiet strength that was her helping me through.

There could obviously have been a bigger biographical outline on my grandmother if I'd had enough foresight to ask her all the questions I have now about her youth passed in England, her marriages, and her opinions on many issues, but I was only a child when she died and it had never occurred to me to interview her while I had the chance. I simply loved and enjoyed her without much thought or examination into the other facets of her life.

Still, there are other amusing accounts of her in Chapter 2-True Short Stories. One is "The Magic Gingersnap", and the other is "Where There's Smoke".

## J.W. Clark

J. W. Clark was like a genie that appeared out of nowhere. One day there was no J.W., the next day he was living with us. No explanation of his presence was given me until I was quite a bit older, but he first came into our lives close to my fourth birthday.

According to the story I was told, he'd been dishonorably discharged from the Navy for I know not what, was out of work and apparently had no place to stay when my parents discovered him sleeping in the garage one night.

One thing I'm sure of without being told is that Earl C. grilled him within an inch of his life before allowing him to be a permanent resident in our home. But that's precisely what he came to be, and once my mother went back to work after I was done with Kindergarten, he was my sole caregiver by day.

To me there was something wary, yet subservient about him whenever there were white people present which for the times we lived in no adult would have thought strange. Yet his responses to my mother were highly disagreeable to me. He called her Miss Jean; reminiscent of the way house servants addressed the mistress of the house. He did most of the cooking and was I thought a better cook than my mother, and also, all of the heavy chores around the house and most of the daily chores while my mother was away at work. Our home had a finished basement which was where he slept and kept all of his possessions which were few. Basically, the housework and care of me was in exchange for room and board.

J.W. Clark was a short, dark complexioned, heavily built man and certainly his experiences were stereotypical of many young black men of that era. He had one face for dealing with his own people, and an entirely different face for dealing with whites. With the idealistic notions that dominate the thinking of most children, I couldn't understand that it was a necessary survival tactic, and was often upset with him for what appeared to me to be groveling or cowardly behavior when he didn't take up for himself.

When summer rolled around after my first year of school, and with both parents working, I was left in J. W.'s continual care which opened up my field of vision into who he was far more than any remarks my parents made concerning him. I noticed on our various errands that his conduct with the white bosses was the same as with my mother. She was good to him, though I felt a little condescending. I didn't understand his servile demeanor in her presence, but it made me angry with both of them. I wanted to see him speak up to her, though in his position it was an unrealistic expectation on my part. It was really equality between them that I wanted to see but the concept was still outside of my mental grasp as were the words to express it.

During the summers, our days started out with him doing the chores my mother had asked him to do before she headed off to work. I'd follow him around the house asking questions that no doubt got on his nerves, but he tolerated me well for one who was unaccustomed to the constant companionship of a small child. He answered me as patiently as he could and when I became too importuning, sent me to the backyard to play until he was finished. Once in a while he would open up and tell me stories from his service in the Navy. But my lasting impression of him was that of a carefully hidden man whom very few, if any, really knew.

Often after his chores were finished, he would call me in to make sure my face and clothes were clean, fix lunch for us both, and then we were off on foot to wherever in the city he could pick up a little extra money on side jobs.

He walked briskly wherever he went and Dandy (the family Boston terrier) and I dawdled along behind him. He had an array of places he visited, all of which were interesting to me because they were unfamiliar. Sometimes it was a small mom and pop restaurant where after talking to the boss a minute he would come out of a backroom armed with a pail and mop to do the floors in which case he always gave me a quarter to play some songs on the jukebox while he worked. I would spin crazily on the split green vinyl stools at the counter, looking at the lacey trails of suds on the floor while I listened to Sixteen Tons by Tennessee Ernie Ford or an assortment of Ray Charles hits.

After the job was done and the money collected, we either went to the drugstore where he often did small jobs for the proprietor or sometimes he took me to the softball games that he enjoyed where behind the fence I would sit in the soft dirt eating a licorice whip or an ice cream cone and watching him play ball.

J.W. had a girlfriend named Belle that whenever time permitted he would visit. She had two children near my age that I played with while they carried on their courtship in the house. I never knew what ended their associations only that after a brief courtship we no longer went to her house. I was sorry to lose my new little friends.

Eventually, he began a new relationship with a woman named Pauline whom after a few years, he married. I was about thirteen or fourteen when he moved out although he continued through the years to keep in pretty consistent touch and participated in our usual family events.

# MILDRED

Mildred was Eleanor's best friend. They became fast friends during the time that my parents decided to entertain at home because interracial couples were not welcome in restaurants and very few bars. Mildred and many others in that ostracized circle attended these parties, but at the advent of my birth the parties stopped, and few maintained their connection after that era ended. Mildred however, continued her friendship with our family.

I remember Mildred from as early as three years old. All of my memories of her are extremely pleasant. I know too much about life now to believe she never had any trouble, but I never heard her complain about anything. In fact, the only time I ever heard her mention her past was one Christmas when I was twelve or thirteen and had spent more than my usual parcel of time with her. We had been out doing a bit of shopping and I noticed that at every opportunity she put money in the Salvation Army buckets. When I asked her why, she told me of a time when she'd spent a couple of years in jail for dating a black man in a state where it was against the law for whites and blacks to associate. She said the Salvation Army came to visit her, and helped her get on her feet when she was released. She said they were the only ones who came at all. That was all she said. No complaints, no accusations, no railing against fate; just the bare bones of the story, and gratitude.

Mildred was glamour incarnate. Her native-American heritage was plain in her face; high cheekbones, dark skin, and onyx eyes that when they were not tinged with mischief or quiet laughter were cool and aloof. Her manner was decidedly aloof, sometimes even bordering on haughtiness if a less genial circuit of thoughts affected her mood. She had a great sense of quiet humor and thoroughly embraced adventure. If there were any shades of lipstick or nail polishes that were either new or out of the ordinary, she had to try them. No matter what she did with herself, she always looked like a Hollywood movie star to us.

She wasn't always talkative but she was good company. Mildred reminded me very much of Clair Bloom as Theo in the movie "The Haunting"; sharp insightful repartee, and she would never let a misconception of anyone else's slip by unremarked. If there were any sleeping dogs, she was going to wake them up...gently, and set them howling. She moved as though she had all the time in the world. I don't recall ever having seen her in a hurry.

Since Mildred lived alone in bachelorette glamour and independence, she frequently let her niece Tracy and me spend the night at her house. There was no news we received with any more excitement than finding out we were going to spend time with her. She had a sassy minor bird with which she had the weirdest conversations, a French poodle, and a cat that was just as aloof as she was. Her vanity table was of particular interest to two young girls approaching the age when we would be allowed to experiment with make-up, and once in a while when Mildred was in the mood, she would expertly do our faces while plying us with questions about school, boyfriends and the like. Usually our stay with her ended in a flourish of riding in her blue Cadillac with the top down to Frankenmuth, MI where we went to a fancy restaurant and afterward walked around the provincial little town peering into shop windows. The trip home was always fun; her glamorous trademark sunglasses and a brightly colored silk scarf trembling in the wind, and Tracy and I laughing loudly in the back seat with our hair streaming behind us and the radio blaring. We felt like millionaires!

## Patsy

Patsy was my first real friend--my best friend throughout our school years and into our early twenties. At that time she disappeared and severed all connections except with her mother whom she swore to secrecy concerning her where-abouts. None of her former friends and classmates has ever been able to figure out what made her leave or why it was so important that she never see or even communicate with any of us again. I've not seen her for thirty years and I often wonder if I will ever see her again this side of the grave. I've missed her and thought of her often—how could I not? We did almost everything together for more than ten years. Every weekend, we spent the night either at her house or mine, we bought matching clothes, played violin together for ten years, got contact lenses at the same time when they were first popular, and I even went with her family to the World Fair in New York City in 1964; and the fixes we got ourselves into would have made some interesting movies. We shared every thought, dream, and bit of nonsense imaginable. And so, even after all these years, I still think about and miss my friend much more than I can say.

Patsy was nearly as fair-skinned as I was; only her hair was red and kinkier than mine. She had startling black eyebrows and nearly black eyes which were able to bore holes in granite when she was angry. In some ways our friendship was really quite remarkable in that our personalities were really very different. Patsy was goal oriented, confident, great in just about everything at school and very pragmatic; whereas I was a dreamer, definitely scholastically challenged except for English and the arts, impetuous, and extremely self-conscious. However, we were marvelously joined at the imagination, and both had a great sense of fun which neatly covered our differences. We rarely had scrapes, and when we did, they blew over quickly.

Patsy seemed to me a complete negative of my own life; well-liked, respected, and in short a valid person in our little circle. Her friendship sort of grafted to me a certain tolerance from our peers. So, I was not only glad of her friendship for the genuine love of her, but I was also immensely grateful for the peace and second hand acceptance that were the pleasant by-products of that alliance. Wherever she went, I went. I knew in my heart that I was invited to many social events for her sake, and her presence definitely dampened if not completely deleted the inherent tendencies of the group to pick on me.

We had such a colorful past that it was a repeated joy to share the laughs with my children who always looked forward to a "Patsy and Stephenie" story. Besides, it's good for children to imagine that 'long ago' their parents were actually carefree kids with mischief on their minds. It almost makes parents human. And so I told them our many adventures, and had as much fun telling as they did hearing. Some adventures were short, others long, but all fondly remembered. Certainly they needed no embellishments. We were well able to get into a scrape without any embellishments from an overzealous script writer.

Some of the more minor incidents included the time right before Christmas when my mother bought a four layer box of very expensive chocolates for the few guests that were expected to drop in during the holiday season. The box itself was extremely decorative and sat tantalizingly on the coffee table next to a pair of Christmas candles. As soon as Patsy and I saw the box of candy, the sin of covetousness entered our eight year old souls, and we knew we were going to have to have a look inside and perhaps have one (or maybe two at the most) pieces of candy. We rationalized that in so big a box of candy surely a couple of pieces gone wouldn't even be noticed. So as soon as an opportunity to be alone with the candy box presented itself, we also happened to be available. First, we tried one. Yuck! Mine was coconut; that doesn't count. Carefully put back into its' paper, you could hardy tell it had a tiny bite out of it. Try again; raspberry cream. Now we're talkin'. Caramels are good! The ones with nuts in them were bad! Before we knew it we were deep in gluttony. Whatever we liked we ate; whatever was nasty was cunningly put back in the box with the bitten part carefully hidden.

I don't think the havoc we wreaked on that candy box hit us until it was over. But one thing dawned on both of us simultaneously as we fell back on the couch with sugar glazed eyes; what was going to happen when my mother found out her candy box had been plundered? Maybe she wouldn't notice. Fat chance of that! Best to leave the scene of the crime immediately.

Neither one of us felt at all well that evening, so I think my mother thought that was adequate punishment for our misdeed, but we did notice thereafter that the next box of chocolates was put on the top shelf of her closet. We would've had to go into her bedroom to get it which wasn't worth what would happen to us if we did.

Elementary school romances are always good fodder for stories and most every family has a few. There was a boy who lived around the corner from Patsy whom we both thought was really cute, and of course stealing a kiss from him was not beneath us. He was a second grader, very large for his age, and as *older women* (we were in the third grade) we were pretty sure it would be hard for him to resist our collective charms, so we just asked him flat out for a kiss. The fact that he was ardently opposed didn't daunt us at all. We refused to take no for an answer. So, since we had already made up our minds to kiss him, kissed he was going to be. The next time he saw us he took off running, but with me being the fastest runner in our school, he didn't stand a chance. We chased him all around the neighborhood until he ran straight into his garage. Cornered! We calmly offered him a second chance to kiss us and while he was still resisting Patsy noticed a book of matches lying on a workbench. She quickly tore out a match and lit it and held it in front of his terror stricken face with the edict "Kiss us or we will burn your nose off." He kissed us, almost sincerely.

Of the two of us, Patsy was by far the more disciplined and self-possessed. She was usually the brain behind our doings with once in a while a suggestion from me. This lack of equality made no difference to me. The uncanny thing about most of the trouble we ever got into was that our two imaginations seemed to grow the same crop of nonsense in the same season. So when we finally got busted for whatever violation, the blame usually fell equally on both of us. Sometimes we learned our lesson early on; other times we got away with our peccadilloes so long that the lesson was a little more painful when it finally came.

One such episode was connected to our love of making erroneous phone calls. We dreamt up many schemes for engaging people in fraudulent conversations. As soon as parents were out of the house or occupied with other things besides spying on us, we would drag out the phone book and find people whose names were funny to us. If a woman answered the phone, we would tell her we were a part of whatever department store popped into our minds, and tell her she had been selected out of a phonebook drawing to receive three, free, black-lace braziers, and that if she would simply give us her bra size, the braziers would be shipped out immediately. I don't know why finding out bra sizes was so entertaining, but it was, and doubtless there were many women watching the mail to receive their gifts, and perhaps confused department stores were receiving calls from those curious women as to where their gifts were.

However, the most problematic phone call we ever made was to the brother of one of our classmates. We were twelve years old, soon to enter the enviable world of teens; in our first year of junior high school, and full of mischief. The said classmate had a much older brother in his early twenties who had a sort of *bad boy* reputation that made him all the more mysterious, and therefore attractive to us.

We were talking about him one Saturday night when my father was out of town and not due home until about nine, and my mother gone on a few errands that would occupy her for a few hours. It was winter and therefore dark by five thirty. We'd been watching television and were pretty bored with it, so, as was the recent trend with us, we decided to amuse ourselves with playing on the phone. I don't remember who thought of it first, but somehow the idea to call our classmates' brother was hatched and so we wasted no time in executing our plan. We looked up the number, assumed our most grown-up air, dialed the number and hoped he would answer. He did. We managed to flirt well enough anonymously. We had so much success that within a few minutes he was going to come over and meet us. Without thinking of the consequences, we actually gave him the address to my house. He lived only a little outside of our neighborhood, so we could expect him in about ten to fifteen minutes.

Initially, we were pretty excited that we'd been able to pull this little charade off; fooling him into thinking we were much older than we were was truly empowering. Not too many minutes went by before it started to dawn on us that soon he would really be standing at the door! He would see that we were not seventeen and eighteen, but twelve year old seventh graders! And on top of that we looked at the clock, and saw that my mother would be home within the hour. That was the scariest revelation of all. And when Earl C. found out he would have no qualms at all about embarrassing us with cussing the guy out and bodily removing him from the house for having the nerve to dare to approach girls as young as we were. The fun of this escapade was instantly over, and our panic was escalating.

At the zenith of our awareness, the doorbell rang. We considered just hiding and not answering the door, but our guilt was devouring us on all sides. This young man had just walked a couple of miles in the dead of winter in pursuit of legal feminine companionship and had no idea of the danger he was in!

We opened the door and there he was in all his sizzling fineness. One look at us and he knew exactly what ruse had been played on him. I believe he decided then and there to get even by teaching the *little girls* a lesson. He walked inside, took off his coat and hat, sat down at the kitchen table, took out a cigarette, lit it, and looked at us shrewdly. It was pointless to even try to continue the masquerade, so we tried to reason with him explaining that we were only playing, we were really sorry, and besides my folks would be home soon! Our guest seemed completely unmoved by our predicament.

The minutes were ticking by. I think he thought we were lying again about my parents coming home soon, because he settled into his chair as if we had a leisurely night ahead of us. By now Patsy was absolutely frantic knowing that not only were we in trouble with my folks, but her mother as well, and even if we could persuade him to leave, there was still the problem of the cigarette smoke in the house. They would think we were smoking and hanging around with older guys, maybe even drinking. We'd be grounded until graduation!

In a burst of pure desperation Patsy grabbed his stylish hat and threw it out into the windy winter night where it was carried halfway down the driveway. Thoroughly exasperated, he snatched up his coat and went out the door after it. As soon as we had locked the door behind him, relief flooded us and we began to erase as best we could all evidence that it had been anything other than an evening like a hundred other evenings we had spent together. Needless to say, this closed the era of telephone pranks for us. Our spirits however were not completely dampened. There were lots of other ways to carry out youthful mischief without using the telephone, and we were bound to find them one by one.

## Mrs. Booker

Mrs. Booker was Patsy's mother and in many ways felt more like a mother to me than my own. It's a sad confession to make but she was much easier to relate to than my own mother was which added to the existing guilt in me concerning her. My mother couldn't help observing my admiration for Patsy's mother and seemed to nurse a sort of guarded, jealous agitation that frequently brought forth the sarcastic remark, "If Mrs. Booker said it, it must be the gospel." Next to my grandmother, Mrs. Booker and my Kindergarten teacher, Mrs. Courts ranked highest in my trust and admiration during my childhood.

Mrs. Booker was an elementary school teacher and the single parent of two children; Patsy and her older brother Bobby. She had great sense of humor but what I most remember her for was her consistent diligence and wisdom in raising her kids and their friends. She was extremely aware of her surroundings and of people; particularly children which I'm sure made her an ideal teacher.

I never saw a more ardent nutritionist or cook. Long before health awareness became all the rage Mrs. Booker believed in eating a colorful diet. I never saw a supper on her table with less than three vegetables, and eating donuts or other breakfast snacks in the morning was seriously out of the question. Once I showed up at their house to ride to school with Patsy, and the first thing she did was interview me as to what I'd eaten for breakfast. When I told her I didn't usually eat breakfast, she indignantly stopped scrapping snow off the car and hauled me into the house where in coat, hat and gloves she dragged out a skillet and starting frying bacon and eggs and making toast. In about five minutes flat I was eating a bacon and egg sandwich on the way to school while hearing a lecture on good eating habits from a provoked woman who seriously believed in the power of a good meal. Thanks to her I've since learned just how important eating for health really is. She made a believer out of me.

Another event that pops into my mind whenever I think of her is the time Patsy and I had gone to a local carnival. We were about thirteen or fourteen at the time and not always on our guard when it came to potentially dangerous situations. While wandering around the carnival checking out cute boys and rides that might be fun or not we were invited to have some *free* rides by a carnie with a smile full of gaps that a hockey player could appreciate. He seemed harmless enough though dirty and unkempt. We giggled and contemplated accepting.

Shortly before we were expecting Patsy's mother to come and pick us up we took one more of those free rides. Unbeknownst to us Mrs. Booker had been waiting in the parking lot taking in the whole scene; us getting on rides without tickets in hand, the carnie flirting, and us giggling about the whole thing. When we got in the car, she let us have it. 'Didn't we know nothing was free? Men expected something for favors?' As light started to dawn on us, we began to feel shame and alarm at how things might have turned out because of our ignorance. At the end of our enlightenment she gave me the choice to tell my mother what I had done or she would tell her. I decided I should be the one. Over the years there were many such lessons I learned from Mrs. Booker as well as times when she was an active advocate on my behalf when either trouble or opportunity came my way.

Though I'd lost contact with Patsy I still visited Mrs. Booker now and again. Up to the end of her life she was as involved as ever helping, contributing, and caring for those around her which has been the hallmark of her life. I miss her very much and think of her often and that will never change!

## Vivian Tripp Wheeland

Mrs. Wheeland was my vocal instructor for nearly eight years. She was probably in her early sixties and was no longer performing when I first met her, but she was an excellent voice teacher and pianist. She was calm and soft spoken and never once did she get angry or short with me in the whole time I was under her instruction.

I owe a huge debt of gratitude to her for her patience and thoroughness. Though I started out in classical music, I eventually became a more eclectic performer singing jazz, pop, folk and show music. Because of the classical groundwork I'd had in training with her, I sing correctly which enables me to do a lot of different things with my voice. In the early years of my music career I sang as many as forty songs a night six nights a week without damaging it. I owe that to Mrs. Wheeland!

She was always willing to go the extra mile to help a student learn and to expose them to as much of the art as was in her capacity to do and then some. Firmly entrench in the techniques she imparted to me, I've pursued a career in performing for the past thirty-three years and am still singing.

Earl & Eleanor C. in the backyard

Mama (in white) Mildred (in black)

Me locked in the yard...but not for long

Esther Jones, my grandmother and hero.

The love of my young life...horses!

J.W.; adopted member of our family and my Caregiver for many years.

Easter-Patsy in yellow...we were 14 years old in this photo

Leon Boyking-Good friend

Kent January-my brother For whom this book was dedicated.

Earl Crompton; UAW Representative

Eleanor's Beauty Salon

Me and Beebee, the wedding gift.

Me at 20...Karl at 3

Nathaniel J. Wilson

Karen

# Brother Wilson

When I think of Godly people, there are many that come to mind, but at the top of that list is Pastor Nathaniel Wilson who probably had the most profound and lasting spiritual effect on my life of anyone I can think of. Though there have certainly been times when I was not in the will of God, Brother Wilson's influence during my spiritual infancy has kept me from losing my balance entirely. Between the Holy Spirit and the zealous spiritual care I had at my beginnings, there is always the knowledge of the truth to stand between me and myself. It reminds me very much of that scripture "Train a child up in the way he should go and he won't stray far from it. " There is real power in knowing the Word of God; unfathomable power in living it.

My spiritual journey began in the backseat of my mother's car when I was only four years old and the search after a connection with God continued until I was an adult. There was never a breach in my thirst, I went from one church to another; one baptism to another; one set of doctrines to another. I wasn't exactly sure what I expected; I only knew that the expectation was unfulfilled and I felt compelled to keep looking.

I felt no particular loyalty to any church or religion. I still don't. I was in pursuit of one thing; the presence of God, and I meant not to stop until I found it. If I couldn't feel God in the church I was attending, I didn't attend it for long. I had a million questions and to date no one had been able to answer them satisfactorily. I often had the feeling that when I questioned ministers it was a little annoying to them and that I should just be a good child and accept their teaching simply because they were the one with the spiritual credentials.

Also, there was the troublesome issue of observing people in the various congregations I'd been a part of. Most of them were in the habit of going to church and yet seemed to lack joy or seemed unable to change undesirable parts of their lives and of their character which I felt they could not possibly be satisfied with. I also felt discouraged that no matter how much preaching I heard in all those different churches, or how badly I wanted to change, I was still unable to conquer parts of my character that were not what I wished them to be. Not that I was stealing, or lying or anything really crazy, but my mind and heart were not under control...more like I was being controlled by them There were attitudes, anger, unforgiveness and other troublesome thoughts and feelings that I wanted to be rid of. It wasn't enough for me just to appear good. I couldn't get away from the idea that if there was truly a God, I ought to be able to feel Him and hear from Him. Without this connection how was I to know with any certainty that He really exists and hears my prayers? Obviously in all the churches I'd attended God was the focal point of preaching and teaching, and yet it felt more like a history lesson; hearing about Jesus did not provide a connection. After all, I'd also been taught about Abraham Lincoln and Napoleon who were real people just as Jesus had once been alive on earth, and yet I had no more connection to Jesus than I did to them. It was very confusing and I began to despair that all I'd ever know of God were the second hand stories people told of Him.

When I was twenty-seven years old, in my second marriage and more disillusioned than ever in my search after God, a friend of ours named James who was a monk invited us to come out for a retreat in the monastery he was a part of in Big Sur, California. We were both pretty excited! These guys were the *spiritual heavies*...right? Surely, these people knew God and with their guidance I would at last be able to find Him for myself.

Not long after the invitation we set out on our trip full of expectation. However during the week we stayed at the monastery, I came to the dismal conclusion that these people were no closer to God than I was. There was a lot of ritual, solitude and prayer, but ultimately no Spirit of God that I could discern. I was never any good at pretending to have something that in truth I didn't have, and once that truth had been recognized I wasted no time in moving on.

When we finally left, James gave us messages to be delivered to a mutual friend of ours in Flint, MI where we lived. The mutual friend was a jazz fan who often came to hear us play; that was how we met him...at a gig. Often James, also a former jazz musician and editor of the notable Jazz magazine, Downbeat, would come out to hear us whenever he was in town and so met many of the people who religiously frequented our gigs. A couple of days after we got home and done with all the unpacking I made good my promise and gave our friend a call.

When I called, his wife (whom I didn't know) answered. I qualified my call immediately lest she think some strange woman up to no good was calling her husband. She also knew James and made the usual inquiries after his health and latest ambitions and also asked how we enjoyed our stay with him. I communicated the details of our trip out west and also my spiritual expectations of the monastery I'd visited which I intimated had gone unsatisfied. She instantly offered a heartfelt invitation to her church. Since I was ever searching and had nothing to lose I agreed to meet her there on the upcoming Sunday.

From the time I walked into the church and especially during the service, I felt what I'd always longed for...the presence of God! I'd never seen people praise God like this; lifting their hands, vocally praising God, weeping, dancing; never had I heard a preacher with such anointing and power! It was just like Harris Temple, the sanctified church I'd grown up across the street from; the vibrant little church my parents wouldn't allow me to attend! It was the little woman in the Baptist Church with the mink she set to flying when her worship overtook her so much that she was escorted into the vestibule until she could regain her composure!! Even as a child I'd known she had something that I wanted, only I didn't know what it was. I'd had peeks into this worship but never had the opportunity to be a part of it! And now, here I was for the first time in the midst of an entire body of joyous worshipers not knowing what to do or where to begin and yet wanting with all my heart to respond to the Spirit of God that I was feeling so deeply! Before I knew it, I was responding and it was the easiest thing I'd ever done, as if I were meant to do it; to join in the worship of many and pour out my heart to God!

On my second visit I was introduced to the pastor, Brother Wilson, who after the service baptized me in the name of Jesus as the Bible instructs us. I'd only ever been baptized in the titles Father, Son, and Holy Ghost, none of which are names. The experience of that baptism was rapturous. In the past I'd participated in baptism only in order to be a member of the specific church I was attending; this however, was very different. This was a cleansing no one could have prepared me for. I was a new creature in Christ! I was asked if I'd ever received the Holy Ghost, but like those in the book of Acts, I had never even heard of receiving it and didn't really know what to expect. But while the choir sang, right in the middle of a Wednesday night service, and almost before I knew what was happening, without prompting or prior teaching I was on my feet praising God with everything in me when all of a sudden I was speaking in an unknown tongue! Skeptical as I had been, I had to believe it. I didn't know any other languages to speak fluently, nor was I trying to imitate those around me, nor had I ever even heard tongues mentioned or expounded on in any of the other churches I'd belonged to in my entire life. Besides, at that level of worship there is only you and God…everything else melts away. Since that experience I've heard many people discredit tongues, saying it was not meant for today's believers but when it happens to you like that, you know it's real!

Brother Wilson welcomed the million unanswered questions I had stored up over the years and patiently answered every one. There were services three times a week and after every service I had my legal pad full of questions that I had saved over the years plus the ones that cropped up in the wake of my new experience in God.

As soon as service was over I would patiently wait for him to take care of any business he might have with the deacons or other members of the congregation. Once he was at liberty and the church empty except for his family, I followed him to his office, my notebook of questions in my hand with the eager expectation of a child on Christmas Eve. Never once did he look at his watch or show any sign of impatience with me. More often than not an hour or two would pass before we came down from the office. There his wife and daughters sat in the unlit sanctuary with the girls often sleeping on the pews while my husband sat on the platform in semidarkness playing the piano while he waited.

Brother Wilson became the father I'd never really had and the most knowledgeable mentor, and spiritual councilor anyone could ask for. Many of the things he shared with me were so far over my head that it would be years before the full import of some of his statements would come to life in my mind. I was insatiably hungry to know the things of God and he fed me generously. I knew that I was taking time from him that could have been spent with his family or resting, but I had to know and this was my chance. The hearsay knowledge I got from listening to the preaching turned into a know-so experience when he took the time to show me where in the Bible these truths could be found so that I could not only know what I believed, but also why I believed it and where in the word of God it could be found.

He was a very charismatic and articulate speaker and when he spoke under the influence of the Holy Spirit you absolutely knew God was speaking through him. No one ever minded a long service when Brother Wilson was preaching and usually the knowledge that we were to have a guest speaker caused some minor disappointment in the congregation since in our eyes no one could approach our Brother Wilson for wisdom in preaching and teaching.

Brother Wilson was deeply loved and respected by the congregation and a year after I came into the church that so changed my life, he was drafted to be the main speaker on an international gospel radio station in another state. When we found out that another pastor would be coming to replace him, it sent a shock wave through the entire church. In fact, he was so well loved that eventually a sizable number of the congregation followed him west to his new destination. He led by example, never looking down on anyone nor making himself out to be someone above the rest; these were the qualities that endeared him to us so much.

Though it has been a little more than a couple of decades since he left, his influence on me has never waned and he and his family remain in my thoughts and prayers daily. A thankfulness that time has not diminished has lived in my heart for a man who took the time I so desperately needed to teach me the things of God and to shed on me a love and patience that has stayed with me through the years and upheld me through many troubles. His words come back to me again and again just when I need perspective or wisdom. It's not that I worship him above God; it's just that he allowed God to use him to light my way and set me on a path I could follow for my whole life and my appreciation continues.

Thanks forever Brother Wilson, God bless you and your family richly!

## Karen

We shared early youth and craziness together. We sort of vaguely knew each other during school and then one night she came into a place where I was singing, tapped me on the shoulder during one of my breaks and started a conversation, and from then on we were best friends.

This was exciting for me since I'd had no real girl companionship since Patsy who'd been the only real friend I'd had through school years had moved away. Karen was to be the friend and sister of the rest of my life.

We were both artists, enthusiastic and mostly starving. She was a wide spectrum artist with creativity invading every cell of her being. Modeling and sewing seemed to take most of her interest and time, though any and everything she turned her hand to was creatively executed and always fun.

I remember one particularly bad year when we were lucky if we ate a good meal once or twice a week. On one particular day of famine the only consumable things at my house were a jug of water, some margarine in the fridge, and a can of Pennsylvania Dutch mushrooms in the pantry. Karen had a can of Thank You brand blueberry pie filling which she brought to my house. Candles were lit; incense was lit and Joni Mitchell was singing philosophical folk songs in the background while we ate the sautéed mushrooms, pie filling and drank the water in some plastic wine glasses while pursuing the meaning of life and love. It was positively "the best of times…"

The main difference between us was that she was much more open to major changes than I was; moving from Flint, MI, to New York City, to Montana; from modeling to ranching. Little by little and over many years her subtle influence has untied some of those OCD knots that controlled my life.

Though geographically we've been separated for nearly thirty years with only brief visits when some event of family would bring her back, nothing has been able to separate our spirits. We've gone through many things together; the births of each other's' children; talked over various child-rearing issues we faced through the years, and the death of Corrie, her beautiful eight year old daughter in a train accident just before arriving in Zurich, Switzerland where her husband who is a Physicist had accepted a teaching post at Zurich University. She answered this most devastating of trials with grace, courage, and strength which I know she was far from feeling at times. Besides love and fellowship I stand in awe of my dear friend. We've both come a long way and the road, however far it stretches before us, will continue to be rich with friendship!

# Chapter 3

# True Short Stories

# The Magic Gingersnap

After much rearranging of two busy schedules to make time for a long desired visit, I finally stood on the porch of one of my closet and dearest friends. When the door opened there was her smiling face! Once the opening amenities settled us warmly into our visit, we reviewed the interval in which we had not seen each other.

The teakettle having been put on shortly after my arrival was now whistling. My friend set a bowl of gingersnaps between us on the table and hurried back to the kitchen to pour the tea. I'd been setting comfortably curled up on the couch but at the sight and the smell of the gingersnaps, I sat up and swung my feet to the floor. Tears of remembrance filled my eyes. I reached out, took a cookie, bit into it and closed my eyes.

Instantly, I was at *her* house, and my senses were flooded with the place! In my mind's eye I could see each room just as it had been when I was last there. Every knick-knack and lamp; the carpet with its' large floral design in muted shades of rose and gray, and the many aromas associated with that wonderful old house were all overwhelmingly present and intact in my memory. Because of my fondness for gingersnaps, the cookie jar stayed magically full during my visits. This and the welcoming aromas of fresh coffee, and meat pies always met me at the door anytime I arrived for a stay. And always, the woody fragrance of my Grandmothers' perfume was for me, an integral part of her enchantment, for it agreeably entered every room with her, and lingered long after she had gone.

There was something magical about that old house. It stood three stories high, the top floor possessing its' own kitchen and porch; and all those stairs and landings between floors were so mysteriously appealing to my childish imagination that I could never resist dallying and daydreaming there.

I remembered a blinking yellow traffic light on the corner of the street where she lived, and late at night while everyone slept, when I would creep quietly out of bed to steal a gingersnap from the large ceramic cookie jar, I recall how unearthly, and yet comfortingly familiar it was to see my Grandmothers' living room lighten and darken to the pulsing rhythm of that light. I would sit in the generous lap of the armchair beside the bay window with my stolen treat enjoying the lightshow, and musing to the loud, steady ticking of the ancient clock on the mantle before I returned to bed. It was to that unremitting tick, and the rich, deep chiming of the hour that I would eventually fall to sleep little dreaming that it marked the golden time of our togetherness, and of childhood, and of life.

Mornings were a favorite time in my Grandmothers' house. It seemed to take forever to fill the old claw-foot bathtub in the bathroom just off the kitchen. Once filled, I floated in my private, sudsy sea, enjoying the warm water until my fingers and toes were completely waterlogged and wrinkly.

After I was dressed, it was off to that marvelous, state-of-the-art-grandma-kitchen. I remember how the sun streaming through the windows lit up the creamy walls, and how Grandmas' cat Tootsie always slept in the sunbeams on the floor. There was never much conversation during meals. The food was too wonderful; talk could wait 'til later.

In the midst of my reverie the sound of cups and saucers being placed on the table broke the spell. I opened my eyes still holding the gingersnap with a single bite gone, and as the slightly worried face of my dear friend came slowly into focus, I heard her ask "Does that cookie seem a little stale to you?"

# Where There's Smoke

There was nothing more exciting to me when I was very young than to hear that we were going to my Grandmother's house for a week or two. In fact my mother never let me know we were going more than a few hours in advance since I would drive her crazy from the time I found out until the time we actually left. Once in the car, knowing we were on our way I would settle down in the back seat and sing every song I knew a dozen times or so until we arrived.

My love of my Grandmother was a mixture of affection and awe. She was a very austere woman, fiercely loyal, but totally intolerant of any kind of nonsense. I answered to perfection the description in the Bible about "nonsense being bound up in the heart of a child," and I knew from past experience what kind of reactions I could expect from my Grandmother if I got busted in the act of nonsense. Talking back, talking when grown-ups were talking, showing out in public would win you a public whipping which at that period of time was more common than not. So, I was very cautious of my behavior when I was going to be spending a lot of time with any grown-up since when you are only four years old the line between sense and nonsense is a little fuzzy. But my grandmother's approval was a highly sought after prize, and so I did my best not to violate her sensibilities.

Once we got to Grandma's house, and the suitcases were unpacked, and lunch eaten, mom and gram made a plan for the afternoon, I only hoped it wasn't shopping. Shopping was the boringest thing in the world to me, especially if I was going to be the purpose for it; being dressed and undressed like a doll for hours on end was not my idea of fun. However, it turned out we were not going shopping, but instead were going to the cemetery which we visited almost every time we went to grandmas; a mysterious place to my way of thinking and one that I entertained many strange notions of concerning the pastimes of the departed while underground.

As usual, I rode in the back seat occupying my time singing, looking out the window and listening to bits of the conversation in the front seat in case anyone said something that was either interesting or understandable to me.

Whenever my Grandmother left the house, she always dressed up whether it was a doctor's appointment, shopping, or a trip to the cemetery. Now dressing up meant brooches, gloves, and a hat, and almost all of her hats had veils which were very sheer and hung anywhere from just below the top rim of her glasses to her chin.

Unfortunately, Grandma smoked cigarettes, a habit that I detested with all my four year old soul, but this wasn't something I was allowed to discuss with her or my parents who also smoked. Part of my fear of her smoking was the fact that she, unlike my parents, (who used matches to light their cigarettes), carried a good sized butane lighter that seemed just a little shy of a flame thrower to light her cigarettes.

While my mother and grandmother talked away in the front seat of the car, my grandmother opened a fresh pack of cigarettes, extracted one, and rummaged around in her purse for her lighter. I watched from the back seat not wanting to miss the mighty flame that would be produced when she flicked it. As I watched, the lighter indeed flicked and its' flame shot up, devouring the veil of her hat faster than you could see and a tiny smoldering flame was beginning right on top of her hat!! I sat forward in the backseat, wildly fascinated and terrified! I knew that interrupting grown-ups was wrong, but even I could see that adhering to this rule under the circumstances might not be the best course of action.

With much trepidation I attempted to interrupt their conversation "Grandma, your…"

My mother never took her eyes off the road but sharply admonished me with "Hush! Don't you hear your grandmother talking?"

By now I was absolutely frantic since I could actually see the little spark on grandma's hat getting bigger and a small thread of smoke issuing from it! In my childish mind all I could think of was, if the whole car got on fire we would all be dead and have to live underground with the folks we were now going to visit!

Without another thought I shouted before I could be shushed again.

"Grandma, your hat is on fire!!"

Instantly two things happened; first my mother slammed on the brakes and next with a shriek grandma tore off her hat with lightning speed and flung it out of the car window probably before my warning had even faded from her hearing.

It was the most empowering experience of my life thus far and my spirit expanded with the climax of this peril. I had taken my young life into my own hands, interrupted my elders, and saved my grandmothers' life all in a matter of seconds. I was the HERO! It was good to be alive!

# Seeds of Disillusion

When I was five years old my attention span for TV heroes was limited since hands down I preferred being outside to sitting still inside for anything. But somehow I met Mighty Mouse and was instantly smitten. Every Saturday morning I would dress up in what I considered romantic clothes, (pink corduroy overalls and a flowered shirt without stains) and sit expectantly in front of the TV to see once again the wondrous deeds of Mighty Mouse. He was fast...he was always on time to save the girl mouse from the evil (and ugly) dishonest John who almost always tied her to the railroad tracks to be squashed to pieces by a train, and on top of all that he had big muscles. He was as real to me as anyone I knew.

For children, falling in love with a cartoon character or examining their impossible realities is part of the magic of childhood! I remember always being completely baffled at the ongoing competition between Popeye and Brutus over Olive oil. To me she was skinny, had chosen a very unbecoming hair style, was silly and had an extremely annoying voice. Why all the fuss over her was totally lost on me. But the little girl mouse was charming and deserved to be saved by Mighty Mouse.

I'm not really sure how many episodes of it I watched before the thought occurred to me that if I were tied up and in trouble, Mighty Mouse would surely come to my rescue. One Saturday morning, to test the heroism of Mighty Mouse, I made myself as attractive as kindergarten skills allow. I got into my mother's knitting basket and borrowed a skein of yarn and ran as fast as I could to my playroom. There, as best I could, I proceeded to tied myself to a chair where I waited a little over an hour to be saved from the fate of boredom if not eminent danger. But alas, no red and blue clad mouse flew into that room. I was heartily disappointed and with a heavy sigh, I slipped out of my soft bondage and went to the kitchen to assuage my disillusionment with a cookie. I still liked Mighty Mouse, but the old thrill just wasn't there anymore. So much for flying heroes.

# When the Law Backs Down

We were late! My dad was rushing around the house trying to remember and locate things my mother had told him to bring out to the lake at Medicine Acres. He'd just gotten in from work and seemed harassed and distracted. In my impatience to leave I followed him from room to room getting underfoot and asking a lot of questions. He shot me an unmistakable glance which any sensible child would have understood to mean they should wait quietly out of his way but I disregarded it. I don't recall the circumstances of why I had stayed behind to come out with him. On days we went to the lake I usually went with my mother earlier in the day and it was dad who didn't get there until after work, so, I was in a big hurry to leave! If he rushed he could get there by six o'clock; still plenty of time in the long summer day to swim and barbecue dinner.

Medicine Acres was the property of a couple of women doctors whom my parents had known for many, many years. Because of the friendship they had extended an open invitation for us to use the cabins by the lake anytime we might wish to. It was a mammoth place and breathtakingly beautiful. The row of cabins was about a stone's throw from the lake which was where we stayed sometimes for weeks at a time. We couldn't see the doctor's home from the lake or any of the rest of the world for that matter. It was like being on a lovely island all alone. We spent every spare moment that could be stolen there during the summers. I loved it especially because when we were there, it seemed like all the troubles in our family, or even the world disappeared.

Today we were late! I was worried to pieces that we wouldn't get there in time for me to play in the water. It would be boring to have to wait until morning. The cabins were small and there was no room to play. Normally, when we arrived early and stayed on the lake until it was dark, I was so exhausted from my ramblings and from playing in the water that I was asleep as soon as my head hit the pillow. But I was not at all tired now.

Finally, we were in the car and on our way although it seemed to me that the trees were going by much faster than normal. We weren't in the car for long before I heard a siren behind us. As my dad started to slow the car down to a stop, I popped up in the back window to see what was going on. Lights were flashing on the car behind us. My dad turned the car off and the door to the car behind us opened. A large and important looking man all dressed in blue got out. He didn't look too happy.

Two things happened simultaneously; first the Policeman bent slightly to get a better look at my dad; he opened his mouth to speak but before either he or my dad got a chance to speak, I poked half of my five year old body through the backseat window, beamed a bright smile at the stranger and said, "Hi! We're goin' to the lake to swim. Can you swim? Dandy here (my dog) can swim real good. Have you got any kids? Can they swim? Are you mad 'cause you're not goin' to the lake? Say, you should go with us! This is my dad. He can swim real good too. Can we go now?"

The officer's demeanor melted from stern to ruefully sympathetic. Then he seemed to be trying to stifle a laugh. Without a word passing between the two men, the policeman turned and walked back to the patrol car. My dad sat perfectly still and then started laughing quietly to himself and shaking his head. He pulled the car back on the road and drove quite a bit slower.
P.S. We did get there in time to swim.

## Big Party! Little Party!

It was a rainy and blustery (which equals boring) afternoon for a four year old who not only couldn't go outside to play, but must also stay out of the way inside since preparations for a small party were in progress. My Grandmother was also visiting which was usually a high point in my life, but today even she did not have time for me as she was helping my mother prepare for the party.

Normally this late in the spring after fine weather had finally arrived, me and my dog, Dandy would have been long gone on adventures throughout the neighborhood. But not today. Dandy, a self-possessed Boston terrier, had resigned himself to dozing in a corner of the living room, while I sat dejectedly on the couch contemplating the unsuitable conundrum of being shut up in the house with nothing to do. Meanwhile, my mother who was hosting the card party was running around the house, dusting, vacuuming, preparing and setting out trays of goodies which I was forbidden to touch. I was promised a treat if I would be good. Though I was a child that usually had no problems entertaining myself, I felt really put out by the shape this day was taking.

"Go play in your room! God knows there are enough toys in there for an army of kids!" was my mothers' exasperated command.

Pouting, I climbed down from the couch, called Dandy, and was on my way to the playroom, when I heard the doorbell ring. Dandy was barking furiously as he did anytime someone came to the house. I could hear my mother and the sound of several other women all exchanging greetings at the same time which gave it a henhouse effect. It made me want to laugh. All of a sudden I was curious to hear what they were saying and doing and realized I would not know what was going on if I stayed in the playroom. Just off the kitchen and down two or three stairs was a little foyer with a coat rack. The kitchen and dining room were separated only by an open archway, so I decided to sit with Dandy on the stairs where I could observe the party unnoticed.

My mother brought a couple of coats and hung them neatly on the pegs and returned to the dining room where the party was now in session. Either she hadn't notice me, or she had no objections to my spying from the foyer as long as I was quiet. By now Dandy after inspecting the coats to see if anyone had smuggled in animals or food, had settled down to continue his nap on the foyer landing.

It the dining room the party was in high gear. Everyone was laughing, and there were mock complaints about the hands that were dealt. The refreshments were greatly appreciated, praised, and ravenously consumed. From time to time my mother would come into the kitchen to refurbish the trays of food, or to bring the collected empty, or near empty beer bottles to put back in their cases that lined the foyer wall.

The party went on all afternoon and into the early evening. More games, more talk, more laughter, more gossip, more food, and more beer. The beer cases were nearly all full in the foyer. As this was the only party treat within my reach and I felt reasonably sure it must be pretty good since so much of it was drunk, and it seemed to make everybody very happy, my curiosity got the best of me, and I began to drink whatever was left in all those bottles. A few drops in one bottle, a third of a bottle in another, a couple of swallows here, and a couple of swallows there until…

From here on I must relate the story as it has been told to me over the years by those who attended the party. Eventually the party came to an end, and my mother came to get the coats of the guests from the foyer when she noticed me passed out on the steps. At first, it was believed that I had just fallen to sleep, until my mother shook me and called out my name loudly and repeatedly. No response. My Grandmother got down to check me out, and then incredulously said "Gracious sakes, Eleanor. The child's drunk!" And so I was. I heard that I never stirred at all that night, and everybody thought I would wake up next morning with a hang over, but instead, I woke up in the best of moods, and mother said I ate the biggest breakfast she had ever known me to eat.

So if you ever have kids, and decide to have a party, 1) Get a baby sitter. 2) Make sure your guests drink ALL their beer; and 3,) Teach your dog to not let your children drink beer.

## A Medical Adventure

In the early spring just a little under a month before my fifth birthday; I sat in the beloved window seat in my toy room chaffing my favorite blanket which was sadly worn. The day was grayish, chilly, and windy. Not a problem for me. I enjoyed watching the squirrels playing chase in the trees and the birds popping in and out of the vines of the neighbors grape arbor just as much as on a sunny, summer day. I was musing and absentmindedly watching the gray clouds ghosting across the sky when it occurred to me that this was not at all a usual morning.

Normally my mother was long gone to work and J.W., my caregiver busy with assorted household chores. But today he was away and my mother was dressed as if to go out on some important errand. The unusual bustling around of my mother and the absence of vacuum cleaners running or other familiar clatter stirred my curiosity. I dismounted my perch in the window seat and went to ask my usual legion of questions.

Entering the kitchen, I saw a green suitcase beside the door which just added to the mystery. I never saw that suitcase unless we were going to my grandmother's house in Jackson, Michigan. Since going to grandma's house was one of my three most favorite things to do, my mother always told me the minute I awoke on such mornings to ensure complete cooperation from me in our preparations to leave.

So far, no one had said anything to me. I heard a noise in the vestibule and ran in to see my mother getting my coat from the closet. She seemed distracted and there was none of the usual pre-travel excitement in her demeanor. I immediately asked why the suitcase was in the kitchen and where we were going.

While buttoning up my coat, she recalled to me how many times I'd been to see Dr. Kingsbury this past winter because of my tonsils, and how sick I had been even at Christmas, and how if I went to the hospital the doctor would take out the offending tonsils and I wouldn't get sick anymore or have to take any more nasty medicine. Most importantly, part of the cure was ice cream...as much as I wanted!

I did remember the unpleasantness of being sick. The nasty medicine however, I had less memory of. Most of the time my mother tried to get me to cooperate by employing the simple psychology of including me in the responsibility of administering my own medication; first, she would pour it into the spoon and then hand it to me. Often though, while she was returning the cap to the medicine and putting it back in the cabinet, I let Dandy, the family Boston terrier, lick the medicine from the spoon. This was my way of including him in my recovery. This could have been, at least in part, responsible for the recurring episodes of tonsillitis.

Once in the car, I continued my line of questioning about the hospital and my soon-to-be extracted tonsils. I'd never been to a hospital before and while I was somewhat hesitant to find out, I was curious enough not to be terrified. When we finally arrived at the hospital I was a little daunted by the size and strangeness of it all. We sat in a couple of chairs while a crisp, professional looking woman asked my mother what seemed to me to be way too many questions while typing away on a typewriter. I felt the tiniest bit indignant. When I asked a lot of questions I was finally told to go outside and play. It looked very impressive though and on several occasions I ventured to ask a few questions of my own but was shushed by my mother.

Finally, all questions asked and answered, a curious looking plastic bracelet, not very pretty in my opinion, was attached to my wrist. While my mother picked up the suitcase, a pretty woman in a dazzlingly white uniform invited me to ride in a chair with large wheels which seemed harmless enough, so I jumped in. We were soon on an elevator, another first for me, which opened after a short ride on a floor equally strange to my eyes. There were children playing in the hallway, and some in rooms that we passed with bags and tubes hanging by their beds; strange smells, machinery and wheelchairs, gurneys, and women dressed in white with sever looking caps fastened in their hair. As long as my mother had me by the hand though, I felt no immediate threat.

At the nurse's desk, my mother spoke in low tones to a nurse who nodded and took us down yet another long hallway to a room where there was a tall bed with plain white sheets. In parting, my mother gave the nurse a few brief instructions, kissed me and told me to be good and do whatever the nurses told me to do until she came back later in the evening after work. Then she unceremoniously left the room.

I was helped up onto the bed by a nurse's aide and my clothes taken off in exchange for some very unglamorous hospital pajamas. The nurse returned a few minutes later to check up on me. Speaking encouragingly as one must when planning to steal the tonsils of a child, she did her best to ease any fears or suspicions I might have by handing me my teddy bear from the open suitcase and smiling warmly at me. She closed the suitcase and took my wrist in her hand while watching her wristwatch and then wrote something on a chart. Next she brought out a needle. These I had seen at Dr. Kingsbury's office and there was the end of my cooperation. She coaxed me for quite a while insisting it wouldn't hurt much. The end result was that I agreed to the shot if she would first give it to my teddy bear. If he didn't scream, then I would submit. He didn't scream, but I certainly did, and I came to the conclusion that these people were not to be trusted. The nurse finally left and I was alone in the big, white, cold room. There were a few animals painted on the wall in an attempt to make the room more cheerful and agreeable to children, but it didn't really lay my apprehension to rest nor curiosity as to what lay beyond my room. As was my habit when left to my own devises, I slipped down from the bed and out of the room unseen to wander and check out the lay of the land for myself.

True to her word my mother returned in the evening to see me and to explain about my tonsils being removed the following morning, but of course, I was not there. The pediatric ward was in an uproar while my mother and the entire nursing staff looked for me in vain. An alert was sent throughout the hospital. After all, how far could a four year old child get in a hospital full of responsible adults?

Hours later I was discovered in the room of a dying, elderly gentleman two floors away. According to the story told me, I was sitting in a chair by his bed, my feet dangling far above the floor in a chair beside the bed and talking to him incessantly. It was said that he had the essence of a smile on his face and probably couldn't have gotten a word in anyway even if he had not been on a journey to the hereafter.

There was a feeling of weak relief among the nursing staff and an extreme scolding from my mother as I was returned to my room, but I had enjoyed my time away and was unrepentant. I was however very sleepy. It had been an unusual day full of new faces and experiences and sleep was crowding my eyelids. Once I was laid down and tucked in with my blanket, my mother's vanishing face and voice reassured me that I would be home with Dandy in no time at all. The last thought I held in my mind before sleep softly obliterated my surroundings, was the promise that in the morning, I could have all the ice cream I wanted. Not a bad trade for the removal of tonsils that were only a nuisance anyway.

## Angels Unaware

It was an unusually hot, sit-in-front-of-the-fan day in the summer of 1977; the kind of day that keeps people in search of something cool to eat or drink or immerse themselves in. Everywhere were aggravated, perspiring faces, not particularly interested in conversation; all bent on some way of cooling off.

I lived in an apartment complex located next to a Seven-Eleven convenience store. My air conditioner was broken along with some other important things in my life, and all my bills were due, and I was deep in the throes of a whopping pity-party when I decided to run over to the Seven-Eleven and grab a cold drink and some ice-cream. Can't have a party with no refreshments.

As soon as I walked in, I knew I'd be there a minute. The store was slammed with hot, thirsty people. Well, I was in no particular hurry, so, I ambled around the store absent mindedly collecting my goodies. When I finally got in the line, it was pretty long, so I returned to the gloomy introspection of my personal affairs and prepared to wait a few minutes. When I'd gotten within reach of the long counter I sat a couple of my things on it. As I stood there staring into space, completely unplugged, I suddenly felt a small hand slip into my free hand. Surprised, I looked down. I hadn't taken notice of the people in front of me; a woman, and a small non-descript child with blond curls and a dirt smudged face. I never did know if it was a boy or a girl.

I'd always gotten along extremely well with children and was never at a loss for words with them; however, today as I looked down into the little face of the child who held my hand and whose eyes held mine with such intensity and purpose that I could not look away, I found no need to speak. The child continued to look up at me, occasionally flashing me the most affectionate smile, all the while holding my hand. We stood there completely contented with the present moment, not needing to speak for what seemed like a much longer period of time than it could possibly have been. In this interval of silent communion my morose mood evaporated as though it had never been.

The woman in front of me had paid for her stuff and was walking towards the door to leave. She looked back to the line to where the child stood still holding my hand and said "Come on. We gotta go." The child looked up at me once again, smiled, let go of my hand reluctantly and walked to the door, looked back once more and smiled, then they were gone.

Of course, I never saw the child again that I know of. But something wonderful happened that day. Somehow our connection became an indelible memory. Not a word was spoken between us; not a word was needed, but the incident became one of those eternal moments that remains alive in your heart for as long as you live.

I went away feeling as though somehow everything would be alright. I received more comfort and encouragement in those few moments than from many lengthy well-meant analytical conversations. I've often wondered if the child received anything from me or if perhaps the child was an angel "entertained unawares". I've wondered what kind of person that child has grown into, and if life has been good to them. I've prayed for that child and most of all remembered vividly and with much gratitude our brief meeting and the way it dismissed my doubts that day.

It's definitely one of my most cherished memories. Whenever my life seems too hard, that memory comes back to me much the way the child did that day; quietly, unobtrusive, undeniably a ministering spirit, and the quality of that moment lives again and as always, I feel encouraged.

## Spontaneous Summer Camp

Being a professional musician was a far different life than I'd envisioned for myself. Though I'd been trained by one of the best vocal instructors in the state for nearly eight years, and was considered an extremely competent artist among my peers it was more a dream of my mother's than it had ever been of mine that I become famous.

Instead of pursuing a music career after high school, I decided I wanted to be a Registered Nurse and so off to college I went for the three year course. A year and a half into the nursing program, my husband was murdered. The emotional trauma brought my life to a complete stand still. Really, I desperately needed a long hiatus to heal and find my way, but life seldom waits for you to get comfortable before moving on. You just have to make your confused way through the fog and somehow do whatever has to be done. At that time my son was only four years old and so I had no choice but to drop out of college and become the family bread winner.

The only thing I was really good at was singing, but introducing myself into that profession was mighty unstable business. So, for the first year until I was better established, I worked two jobs; Secretary of State from nine to five, five days a week and I sang in lounge acts from nine until one, five or six nights a week. My energies were taxed to the limit just trying to say alive financially during those two years while also dealing with the emotional upheaval my life had been for so long. My nonstop work schedule was so featureless I have few memories that stand out of that segment of time. Thankfully, it didn't take too long before word of mouth soon gave me a respectable following; good enough to make my way in the entertainment industry without the necessity of a day job. This freed me up so that I could use my time and energies for refining my performance and adding new materials.

I lived in an agreeable community of townhouses which had quite a diverse population. My neighbors were Hispanic, Oriental, Black, White, and quite a few deaf people. I couldn't think of any living situation that could have pleased me more! Most of the people living there were regular folks with nine to five jobs which left the complex pretty empty during the day. My own son was involved in summer programs or at the grandparents during part of each day, so I used my free afternoons to practice music. Since I had the freedom of the castle, I could practice without disturbing anyone.

One afternoon, not many days after school was out for the summer, I was in my living room as was my habit this time of day, running over vocal exercises and songs. I usually left the front door open and all the windows to enjoy the welcome summer breezes.

It was a gorgeous day with a gentle wind and I was really into the song I was singing when during a rest in the music I thought I heard a noise on the front porch. I paused to listen, but since it was not repeated I dismissed it as probably someone's pet passing by and went back to singing. A few minutes later I heard it again. My curiosity piqued, I got up and went to the front door to have a look around. To my utter amazement there were more than a dozen kids clustered on and around my porch. They ranged in ages four to thirteen representing the various ethnic groups in our neighborhood. They didn't jump up and run away but instead looked up at me expectantly. One little girl timidly spoke up in a sweet, childish voice saying "We were just listening to you sing. You sing really good!"

Warmed by their praise, I smiled and asked how long they'd been listening and she said that since school was out (about a week) they'd come every day to hear me. I was deeply touched by their interest and patient silence. I thanked them, told them they were welcome to stay and then went back inside to my work.

Within a couple of days, more were added to their number. They came at about noon and stayed until they had to go home to their dinners half a dozen hours later. I wondered about it a lot. There wasn't anything for them to do hanging out on my porch most of the day, silent and fasting. It bothered me and I felt I should somehow respond to their patient interest.

Next day, I invited them in and they sat around the living room listening to me practice. I took more breaks than usual asking questions and answering theirs. Within the week they had gotten quite comfortable and adoring and ask if they could help do things for me, dishes or whatever. Also, their parents seemed to have heard of their new daytime activities and decided that it was a boon to have the children in the safe environment of a neighbor's house while they were away at work. They began to send their children with money to help out with lunch which was great since I didn't have the means to feed so many children.

Every day along about two o'clock I took a break from singing collected the cash offerings the children brought with them and after a short council about what we should have for lunch, our group traveled like a small caravan to a neighborhood grocery store for sandwich materials and milk and cookies. I'm sure that many in the area who got used to seeing our daily procession wondered whether a new summer camp or orphanage had opened up nearby. The people in our way always greeted us with amused smiles and friendly greetings.

When we returned from our daily outing, everybody got involved in getting the lunch ready and in cleaning up after which made the process go smoothly and quickly. I was so impressed with how well they obeyed and how anxious they were to cooperate in whatever was going on that I devised a reward system. I collected all sorts of interesting, second-hand things in a chest; old purses, sets of ball and jacks, old jewelry, boxes of crayons, and coloring books, kites and anything else I could think of. When someone had been particularly good they were allowed to choose something from the chest. Though only rarely were any of the things new, it didn't matter to them at all.

Among our number there were two deaf children; one of whom would never attempt to speak. Since much of my vocal training had to do with the study of the execution of vowels and consonants similar to speech therapy, I was able to work with them a little on the mechanics of speech. It actually worked, and whenever they pronounced a word we'd been working on, they were rewarded with a choice from the chest. We also turned up the bass on the stereo so that they could feel the beat of the music through the floor and with beaming eyes and smiles they danced along with the rest of the kids.

The summer sped quickly by with these pleasant occupations and school once again resumed which brought an abrupt end to our daily schedule. It felt a little sad and empty, but it was a sweet chapter in my life that I look back on fondly and often.

## Pets and Parents

Skipping ahead to the time when my own children were young (ten, eight, and five years old), we'd just moved into a townhouse that for the children must have seemed more like a cage after living in the country for so many years. We were all trying to adjust with the proper attitude to incredibly cramped living quarters after the luxury of living on the back of a two hundred and three acre horse farm. Our home had been surrounded by ten acres of forest, and our nearest neighbor on the other side a quarter of a mile away. The townhouse had all the charm of living in a commune.

The adjustment was harder for the children who had to calm down their wild play, and be more aware of the noise they made because of the closeness of neighbors. All these tedious adjustments set their minds working on a solution, or should I say a compensation for their new hardships, and it wasn't too long before they came to the unanimous conclusion that a pet was a sufficient remedy for their sacrifices.

One evening they came in a body to speak to their father and me about the possibility (and advantages) of a pet. Because of the precociousness, unusual eloquence, and diplomacy of the five year old, he was always elected as spokesman for the committee. He had an untarnished reputation for success in similar negotiations. The upshot of that meeting was that their Dad was completely against having a dog in so small a place but at last capitulated to the idea of hamsters which could be kept in a cage and more importantly, out of his sight.

Next day, the kids and I took a trip to Meijer to see what the pet section had to offer in the way of hamsters and were rewarded in finding two very cute ones which we purchased along with all the trimmings to create a hamster paradise, wheels, tubes and all. The children were ecstatic, and we assumed the hamsters would be sufficiently satisfied in their new domain.

We got them home and their cages fixed up and set on top of the children's dresser, and of course named; Miss Mouse from the Secret of NIMH, and Stuart Little from the famous children's book by E.B.White. Everyone seemed pleased with the arrangement. The hamsters were watched with great interest and occasionally taken from their cage to ride on Fisher-Price fire trucks or set free in my daughter's doll house to poop in Barbie's kitchen or bedroom as they inspected every tiny room.

In due time as must be expected, our hamsters (as in Noah's day) being male and female were expecting. At first it was sort of exciting, and I even thought it would be a worthwhile experience for the children to observe the parenting skills of their pets and to enjoy the cute antics of half a dozen or so tiny new hamsters. But as with any growing family, the problem becomes the necessity for more space, so when the babies got some size on them we bought another cage and tried to separate the girls and boys, which unless you're a hamster expert is a little confusing.

We made the inevitable mistake, and as a result, two more hamsters were in the family way and at this juncture of pet/family relations, the children's father took it on himself to build a hamster complex for our colony of rodents outside on the back porch. This may have been done in the hopes that the neighbor's cat would thin the population. Among the newly born hamsters was a white one who was blind probably from inbreeding and we were sure it was a female, so we named her Selena for the lead actress in "A Patch of Blue," whose character was blind. Again we separated the boys from the girls. Again, we made a mistake. Selena (the blind female hamster) turned out to be blind Bartemaous of the scriptures, and since sight is immaterial in reproduction, he impregnated every hamster in the cage.

By the time we took a census of the generations of hamsters in our care, their hedonistic lifestyle of eating, drinking and bringing forth had furnished us with some sixty head of hamsters; way more than were ever in our plans to deal with. It was definitely time to pass some of our increase on to other deserving families.

As soon as the most recently born hamsters were old enough to make their way in the world, we began to offer them to the local pet stores who took them for free which was fine with us. We got the general population down to fourteen hamsters; still too many. I was determined to get back to our original number of just two. Twelve more hamsters to get rid of. What to do?

The following day, I had to go to Meijer to get hamster food and bedding and while I was there I noticed a couple of hamsters loose on the floor and heard the women who worked in the pet department shrieking as they ran by her feet. Later as she waited on me she complained about how the hamsters were finding ways to get out of their cages and that she wasn't going to touch them to put them back even if she lost her job there. Since I wasn't afraid to handle them, I picked them up and returned them to their cage to her utter relief, and it seemed to me in that instant that the answer to my problem was at last clear!

I spoke to no one about my plans until I had my strategy completely worked out. Since it was the week-end, the kids stayed up as late as I did. Along about mid-night I told them my plan and while they were doubtful as to whether I could actually pull it off, they thought it would be good times to watch me try. By the time we had talked it over and laughed about the possible obstacles and outcomes of this tricky operation it was well after 2:00 am. I chose this hour of the night because it would mean fewer witnesses or obstacles to my plans.

I went to my closet and grabbed a very large and slightly shabby black purse and emptied it. Then I loaded it with the twelve surplus hamsters who were none too enthusiastic about inhabiting a purse with no food and no wheel. We all piled into the car with a great sense of adventure. I entrusted the purse to my oldest son so that I could pay attention to driving. When we pulled into Meijer's parking lot it was close to 3:00 am and luckily there were very few cars in the parking lot.

We all got out of the car and the purse was handed to me. I was definitely on my own now. The kids didn't even want to be anywhere near me in case I got busted, so they followed at a safe distance. By this time the hamsters had had enough of being confined in a purse and began to wiggle and squeak. I had to stay as far away from people as possible since it was getting harder and harder to subdue my writhing purse which would certainly arouse suspicion. I slunk around each corner taking a circuitous route to the pet aisle to avoid discovery; my children not far behind giggling and poking fun at my predicament.

Finally, I was where I needed to be, and thanks be to God there was no one else nearby! All the cages had shades drawn for the night, and since people normally did not purchase pets at this hour, no employee was needed in this section of the store. Quickly I unloaded my cargo on the floor. The hamsters thrilled to be free again began investigating their new surroundings. I left the area at once in search of anyone who worked in the store.

The first employee I found was a woman straightening up some plants in the garden section. I explained to her that while I was shopping for some pet food I'd seen some hamsters loose on the floor. She shook her head in exasperation and said they were always getting loose and that she would have to go and find someone willing to put them back. If they thought she was going to do it, they were crazy! At this point I said she needn't trouble herself. I had hamsters and was used to handling them. If she had no objections, I'd be glad to put them back for her. She didn't hesitate to take me up on the offer just as I had intended. As I captured and installed each little hamster into a cage, I said a silent farewell. The employee and I exchanged a few more pleasantries, and then I picked up a bag of hamster food and headed for check-out.

By now, the children joined me, slapping me on the back for my cunning success. Of course, they felt a little sad at the loss of some of their livestock, but the humorous adventure of getting rid of them gave balance to the situation. We were now back to two hamsters, who lived happily ever after until the end of their little rodent lives.

Thus ended the dynasty of hamsters under our roof.

## Double Jeopardy

Does it ever seem to you that the most harrowing family adventures happen in the late PM or the early AM hours of the night? You know, babies born in the middle of the night; a cat that once fell squalling down the chimney in the dead of the night, scaring the family half to death; assorted trips to the Emergency room, and miscellaneous events that quicken the heart and raise the blood pressure.

Well, once upon a summers' eve, my middle son, Nathanael, who was almost fifteen and had a job bussing in a restaurant a few miles away called very late at the end of a large and long special party. His ride home had had to leave much earlier than usual due to some family emergency leaving him stranded at work, and the restaurant was going to be closing within the hour.

I was totally unprepared for taxi service. My daughter Erica and my youngest son Nicodemus were home with me and their father was out of town with the family car. The only other car available was a '69 turquoise Mustang in the driveway that needed a lot of work, and anyway it was a stick shift. I had a blurry, unpleasant memory of driving a stick long, long ago and knew I wasn't up to the task of attempting to drive one at this late date. However, Nathanael was going to be out of work soon many miles from home, and it was late.

Nicodemus, my youngest at nine years old, proposed that there was really not much to it. After all, his father had been teaching him how to drive a stick, and we all had tremendous respect for his learning abilities ever since he'd memorized and perfectly recited the preamble to the constitution when he was two and a half years old. He admitted that because of his size, working the clutch would be a problem, but felt sure that if I handled the clutch while he did the stick, the thing could be done. Really, he was so reassuring, that I finally consented. And after all, there were no other options.

We headed out to the car only to find that the seat was stuck so far back that even I couldn't reach the clutch with my foot. Back in the house we went to get a pile of pillows to put behind me. Finally we were situated in the car. It was a good thing we were on back roads for most of our journey. I can only imagine the comedy this spectacle presented as we halted, lurched, and jerked drunkenly down the road back and forth between first and second gear. We sweated over every stop sign.

The real fun came when we got to the main roads where there was a fair amount of traffic to deal with. We prayed continually for the lights to stay green for us so we could just coast along in third or fourth gear where our disability was a little less noticeable, but we would inevitably catch red lights where we had to go back to first and second gear again which we did none to smoothly. People laughed at us, cussed us out, and sped around us shaking their heads at the stupid lady who couldn't drive.

When we pulled into the restaurant parking lot which seemed like an eon later, I felt like we had mastered some remarkable feat. I wasn't particularly excited about a repeat performance, but at least now I knew it could be done, although I was sure the transmission was being destroyed in the process.

Nic was disappointed when I ended up seeing an old friend also leaving the restaurant, who after hearing our story about the ride to the restaurant offered to let us follow him in his car while he took the Mustang home for us. He did not have to ask twice! And if that car is any kin to Herbie of Disney fame, it was also breathing a sigh of relief! From that time to this I have never driven another stick shift.

# Chapter 4

# The Perilous Solitude

## Responses from the Wounded

At the beginning of writing this book, the horrific Virginia Tech murders happened to us. I say us because when anything of this magnitude happens in what we think of as a safe place, among what we think of as decent people, it affects everyone. We hear of these gruesome and unimaginably brutal incidents in the news over and over again with alarming regularity. The exploding, internal battles of frustrated, disillusioned people no longer able to contain their anger and pain fills the news, our conversations, and our uncomfortable private thoughts in the wake of such devastation. The dismantling of our false sense of security wakes the question "Could anything have been done to have prevented this?"

Society is quick to expiate itself from any culpability concerning these self-destructing people. The blame solely belongs to the demented individual or to the parents and environment that produced an unstable character whose surprise behavior has now become the problem of a select few (the victims and their families', prisons, and psychiatrists) and that's if they don't kill themselves before being taken into custody. There's no doubt that parents make mistakes, or are sometimes even willfully negligent or cruel which over time will to varying degrees erode the spirit of a child, but I believe there's plenty the rest of us could do to diffuse the volatile natures of those we may meet in everyday life upon whom caring and simple kindness may have a healing effect.

I'm always intensely amazed by the sincere shock people express following each new report that yet again someone has just lost it and done great harm to others and themselves. Over and over again during the reports of the Virginia Tech murders, I heard the comments of those who were in the vicinity of this sick and tormented young man. As I watched accounts of this young man's life and those who spoke of him, it seemed that his *strangeness* was a source of amusement for some of the students not at all unlike scenarios I'd witnessed up close and personal in elementary school where the different child is continually taunted and excluded by the clique. However, one would think in a university of higher learning (and it is to be hoped, thinking) that it just might occur to students and professors that it's dangerous business to consistently exclude, push away, or deride a fellow human being. Yes, we all have our favorite people and only so much time and energy to spend on them, but kindness is not time consuming; it's wisdom, and an excellent way to invest in a safer society. An unloved, disconnected human being is a social liability; extremely dangerous as any creature might be that is in more pain than can be endured.

I've watched from my own solitude the one dimensional, mass mindset that passes for awareness. It's not usually intentional or malicious, just a self-centered unawareness. Most of us would run to a person who was lying in the street bleeding whether friend or stranger; ship food overseas to the poor, or respond to any other extreme situation of physical want or need. We will help them get *stuff*, which is not without merit, but so many of us don't *feel* those around us or see sadness and desperation in their eyes, or hear loneliness in a voice. The truth is, loneliness is not just fodder for romance novels, it is a real and dangerous epidemic among us and it kills as surely as any bullet. People die emotional deaths every day in the presence of many who never really see them. We only seem to wake up in the aftermath of their pain.

There should be some desire in us to want to help prevent these emotional suicides. The emotional maintenance of those around us would be much less costly than coming to the uncaring conclusion that it's not up to us as individuals to worry about the lonely isolation of another. We don't have to form costly organizations to solve these kinds of problems. All we have to do is care. Being our brothers' keeper is a spiritual responsibility that when answered in the affirmative edifies both the keeper and the kept.

When my children were very young, we would sometimes be out running errands and occasionally, perhaps at the bank or the grocery store, have to do business with a very unpleasant and grouchy person. Our first response to someone like that is to snap back at them: our first opinion of them is that they are just a rotten, ill-humored person who should be reported to the manager or in some way put in check. At a glance, being on the receiving end of such an encounter, most would favor or even enjoy a tit for tat response believing that the other person started it and had it coming. But I think it's wiser to have a second look.

Early on in my life my opinions were softened and even my most harsh response was not wholly without mercy when I would encounter a mean-spirited person. I believe my own solitude helped me interpret with a little more tolerance these prickly and very unpleasant folks. Those lucky enough to have never had to deal with being excluded are sometimes unimaginative when it comes to empathizing with those who are. I told my children that whenever they met someone who seemed unreasonably hateful, that it was a symptom of that person's unhappiness. Happy people, loved people, people who have meaningful connections and purpose do not behave that way. Those whose wounds are showing in their disagreeable behavior are people we should go the extra mile to really see and be kind to in spite of their recalcitrant manner. None of us knows the heaviness another might be carrying around in his heart and mind. I've found that looking into the eyes of the person I'm speaking with, signifying that for this period of time we are connected; that for me they really exist, and genuine simple kindness disarms even if only for that small space of time, the venom that has accumulated in them.

I know how much it's meant to me during times when I felt disconnected and worthless, to feel real kindness from another unsuspecting person. In that moment it was enough to stand me back on my feet and help me go on a little farther. Simple acts of kindness and warmth are truly lifelines to those who are drowning emotionally. Never underestimate your power to save by simple acts of kindness!

In our culture we believe we've done our duty if we've not overtly rejected or insulted someone…so careful to be *politically correct.* But being politically correct and abiding by the social amenities in no way means that we have done enough. Being tolerated and not insulted are not the same things as being accepted, or being acknowledged for the worth in us. How well I understood that even as a child. There came a point in time when I was no longer chased home with rocks and bad names hurled after me. As a child I'd always thought how wonderful a day it would be when those bad things stopped happening to me. I was sure it would be the end of my solitude and the beginning of belonging. But when they did stop, I was chagrinned to find out that I still didn't have what I needed so desperately. Being tolerated, even though it was a giant step up from being persecuted was still not enough to answer the need. It doesn't quite matter whether the distance between two people is an inch or a mile…it's still not a connection. Only acceptance and connection would help me believe in myself. Without connection we can mutate into a number of unwholesome entities.

People who are isolated and have no outlet for their emotions, nowhere to share themselves, nowhere to spend their love or their gifts are dangerous people. Many will not go quietly into the night. In the struggle to believe that they matter, (when all the while their daily ostracism tells them they don't) it becomes more possible that their hurt could overflow and damage those around them; in their mind a fitting punishment for the ones responsible for their societal exile. When someone is consistently treated with inhumanity they in turn are unable to see those who have slighted them as human which makes it much easier for them to be destroyed en mass such as happened at Virginia Tech. Let us be human with each other!

It's not just these mass school killings that are greatly publicized and hurt so much, but all the private suicides which leave those connected to the victim wondering for a lifetime what they could have done to help. I lost a brother to suicide. Even though I hadn't met him until he was in his mid-teens and I in my early twenties as we were not raised together, it still hurts me that I minimized the problems he was dealing with. I was so certain that after all he'd gone through that the seemingly small event of a failed relationship was nothing he wouldn't get over. I was wrong. Sometimes it's not the big things, but the proverbial straw that breaks the camels' back that needs to command our attention and action. Instead of brushing over his hurt because it upset me (certainly there was nothing I could do about his loss) still, I ought to have sat down with him and let him pour out the hurt and frustration verbally, in tears or whatever. I ought to have put my arm around him and encouraged him that things would be better and not to lose heart. He kept his pain to himself not to bother anyone with it, and we let him because it made us uncomfortable because it was awful see him so hurt and we believed there was nothing we could do to help…and that was the killer.

The suicide of a relative or friend leaves an unclean wound that though it does lessen in time doesn't heal thoroughly as a natural death would. Its scar is forever. It only makes sense to be aware of others; family, friends and strangers. It's worth it to take the time to notice and minister to another's pain instead of rocking along unaware only to be torn from your slumber with the news of a suicide, one that had you been aware you would have seen coming. The careless disregard of and the erroneous notion that the pain of others is not our concern is a deception that too often abruptly ends with violent responses from the emotionally wounded; the bi product of our negligence.

Today thousands are left to grapple with the sorrow and deep wounds inflicted by one sad and isolated young man who lost his battle to be someone special. It makes me wonder how differently his life would have played out if he'd had even one friend to talk to about what was happening to him inside. Maybe if he'd had a friend to share life with there wouldn't have ever been a problem to remedy. Certainly there is responsibility for the deaths of those innocent few that lies with the people who deliberately pushed this young man away and took pleasure in making him feel like an outsider. They lit a fuse and unwittingly watched it burn to the point of explosion.

God once asked Cain about his brother, Able, to which Cain answered, "Am I my brother's keeper?" Whether we like it or not, the answer to that question is yes. I'm afraid that until that answer is fully understood and acted upon, we will continue to see the violent outcome of those who have come to the conclusion that lives, both theirs and others, have no value.

## Drawbacks of Solitude

Finding ways to share at least some of what you feel is essential in keeping your balance in solitude. I found that keeping journals was very helpful to me. Those in solitude go through the same assortment of emotions that everyone does without the benefit of interaction. This is unbelievably frustrating and in my opinion if not alleviated in some satisfactory way leads to such bitterness in some people that their chances of exiting that solitude narrows considerably; in others the accumulated, unexpressed feelings explode in acts of violence.

In this day and age there are a few social venues the internet offers like Facebook and other such links where you can post your feelings, pictures, interests and other bits of information which allows people to get a look at you from a comfortable distance and perhaps realize that they may be mistaken in their suppositions. The most imposing drawback of the ostracized is the erroneous presumption that your difference must be a negative.

A priority in withstanding solitude when we'd desperately rather be part of something or a particular circle of people is not to allow the rejection to define us. That is precisely what happened to the young man in the Virginia Tech murders. Not that everyone who's in an unwanted solitude will eventually become angry enough to punish by murder anyone who shut them out of the human race, but there are never the less levels of damage that affect us deeply and sabotage our abilities to respond correctly when opportunities of socialization finally present themselves.

I'd say the worse drawback in solitude is that many who have suffered loneliness over a long period of time are more likely to allow people into their lives who may not be the best influence or who knowingly prey on their vulnerability. The isolated one may blatantly ignore red flags they see in the newcomer's behavior that clearly warns them to steer clear of a relationship of any kind with someone who is cruel, inconsiderate, unaware, or domineering. But so deep is the need for companionship that many times questionable behavior is overlooked just for the reprieve of breaking up the long droughts of eating alone, sitting alone, walking alone, laughing alone, crying alone, sleeping alone day after day, after day, after month, after year. The sad thing about enduring bad company is that when we allow someone with an unscrupulous character access to our emotions we are no closer to getting what we need from them than we were before we let them into our life. They are not interested in meeting needs.

Those who recognize the deep hunger to belong in someone and target them for emotional exploitation seem to understand by osmosis that they will not be called into account very often by those that need them. Whatever has caused enough damage in them to foster such insecurities that they need to control and manipulate others in order to keep at bay their feelings of powerlessness and unworthiness is what fuels them to find one even more needy than themselves. It's an ugly cycle; on the one hand, a lonely person who needs a connection; on the other hand, an equally damaged person whose only way to validation is to invalidate another. To their way of thinking, to validate you is to lose the upper hand in the relationship. For such a person relationships are not about equality and sharing; they are about power and control. Someone has to be on top, and however much invalidating they have to do; they will be on top, even at the expense of your mangled spirit.

Whether you're a loner or a socialite, if there's anyone among your connections who invalidates you frequently, you need to gird up the loins of your resolve and lose them; people who don't believe you when you share something with them, or who are continually minimizing your experiences either of sorrow or victory are also minimizing you.

There was once someone in my life that I loved with all there was in me and whom I trusted, which for me was the hardest accomplishment, but who refused ever to let my head be higher than his. If he were thrilled, I should be thrilled. If I was thrilled first, then it would instantly be taken away. He just had to control the amount of joy I received. I came to understand that my happiness's and achievements were somehow viewed as threats by him.

Many times when I would confide something that troubled or hurt me, he would remind me of all the horrors of this life from the Holocaust to Hurricane Katrina and made to feel I had no right to the emotions I was experiencing, and therefore would receive neither empathy nor comfort. Certainly I never compared my woes to those horrific events, but I have always believed that even our smallest issues of skinned knees, broken hearts, and disappointments while not earth shattering, are still valid. I believe that is precisely why God provided us with mothers and fathers, spouses, siblings and friends, so that there would be someone to whom our little pains would matter; so that no one would have to go through this life alone  He provided us with people who are in a position to care specifically for us even if the whole world falls apart. Sometimes there's not much we can do to soften the blow for those we love. But one thing we can always do is care. I said as much to my partner, but as usual, he wasn't listening.

Another drawback is that it's possible to stop believing in yourself since there is no one to affirm you. In solitude it is important to learn to care for yourself as you wish someone else would. Just because you are alone doesn't mean you can't or don't deserve to experience kindness. It doesn't mean that you are somehow unworthy to merit companionship. Be particular about who you let into your world with the same vigilance you would exercise over a young and vulnerable child you didn't want getting mixed up with *the wrong crowd*. Be kind to yourself, and as forgiving as you would be to another. Know that your solitude is not the verdict for being unworthy, but rather the by-product of fear and ignorance which have damaged society as a whole. Have faith in yourself, that your life has meaning which no one can diminish. And most and hardest of all, be patient. It really is better to be alone than to be emotionally ravaged by unwholesome relationships.

Yet another inconvenient thing about too much solitude is that we lose the knack of being with others. Sometimes we tend to feel awkward and out of place in social settings. It's not exactly an illusion. People who inhabit solitude are, in fact, different. There's no way you can spend the bulk of your life alone and not have it change you, especially if it was imposed because you were perceived as being different. Inhabiting a country all by yourself makes you the sovereign, the subject, the ogre, and the town wise man all in one. Sometimes, you hardly know how to respond when you encounter others. I like to think of myself as considerate in that when alone I consider many people and situations. Yet when someone came to my home, because I had been so unused to company, I might forget as simple a thing as offering them a beverage. This can start an avalanche of misunderstanding. The person you failed to offer a glass of water may because of regular associations assume you are self-centered and without manners while in your reality they'd be as welcome as Christmas to any reasonable request they asked of you. Many times I've had people a little put out with me because it seemed to them I should have stepped forward and offered to help, perhaps in the decorating plans for a wedding or party; or to have stepped forward and spoken to someone in regards to a job or whatever, but because so early I had been rebuffed so brutally when trying to step up to offer myself as a friend or to offer my services, I came to be someone who steps forward only if I am asked. In solitude, more often than not, the ability to be assertive has been sorely impaired if not altogether disabled.

One of my most treasured pastimes in solitude is reading. I do *a lot* of reading. In solitude, my chums are the characters in the books I read. Consequently, in spending a lot of time with anyone, you will pick up euphemisms and other bits of their speech, and if you are around folks of a different culture in your reading, you might even be feeling a little Irish or Jewish or whatever, and a hint of that gets grafted into your speech. Honestly, I've caught myself on numerous occasions responding to someone in the same vernacular as one of the characters in Dickens's novels or whatever other literature I was reading at the time. These kinds of conversational anomalies are certain to raise some eyebrows and certify your weirdness in the eyes of those you're speaking to. It's provided a few laughs and many questions into the reason for unusual habits of speech I may have employed; some thought it quaint and interesting; others just thought I was some weirdo acting out, but for me it was just the natural result of being alone with my books.

It's very important not to be buried in your solitude; keep yourself informed about what's going on in your city, your state, and in the world as much as possible so that in your occasional social interactions there is something current to talk about. During brief exchanges of commonality many friendships have begun. And always remember, believing in yourself is the best means of inspiring others to believe in you.

One very obvious drawback to solitude is that since you're always alone, you can pretty much have things your own way: no need to compromise; no need to please anyone but yourself. It's easy to get stuck on your own way of doing things that could perhaps make it a bit difficult to lose some personal freedoms but give and take is a wholesome part of companionship. It may take a conscious effort in deferring to the sensibilities and preferences of others, but most of the time it's well worth it.

Still another drawback of solitude that deserves a few words is that sometimes those who have been alone frequently over time may develop a disregard for their personal appearance. Why take a lot of time to be presentable? Why get up in the morning and shower, shave, wear cologne or worry over your hair and clothes?

There's no one there to care or even notice our efforts to be visually pleasing; it only seems to enhance the loneliness to be all dressed up with no place to go and no one to notice.

I can't stress enough how important it is for you to take good care of yourself physically and see to it that you look and feel your best whether anyone notices or not! Though it seems like a vain effort, do it for yourself, because you matter. In solitude we tend to deal with feelings of unworthiness because we've been rejected by others. If we're not careful, we will eventually succumb to their idea of who we are. Just because someone else doesn't quite see your value doesn't mean you have none. It's vitally important to retain and protect a positive view of yourself through good grooming and healthy lifestyle choices.

# Chapter 5
# Observations in Solitude

## Observations

It's really awful if you can't find some privileged moments in the disadvantage of being an emotional outsider. Really, a very decent (and sometimes quite entertaining) education can be got just from paying attention to what's going on right under your nose. Most of the time being somewhat invisible was highly instructive, and sometimes it was just plain annoying or heartbreakingly sad because from where I was standing, the problems were remediable, with patience, effort, and just a little imagination. But the observations I was able to make have always been useful in expanding my awareness no matter what arena of life they occurred in.

Since it would be a book in itself, hundreds of observances are going to be left out, but these few were recurrent and became top shelf awareness's for me and so I will share them.
In regards to parents with children:
1.) Whether in church, restaurant, or events like weddings, I've watched parents wrap up their infants in sweaters, snowsuits, hats and mittens, and then cover the poor little child in a car seat with a large Winnie the Pooh quilt blanket and then spend a half hour leave-taking and chatting here and there as they slowly exit the scene. Meanwhile the unfortunate child is being steamed like a broccoli in his car seat.
**Suggestion:** Say good-bye first, and then wrap the child up…remember the child is alive!

2.) One thing I've witnessed with infants and their parents which is extremely funny, but rude, are parents who wake up in the morning and grab their little bundle of joy and start kissing their face, singing little nonsense songs and talking baby talk with morning breath. What could anyone do in a situation where they are being held a bare inch away from a really foul smell by someone ten times their size except turn their face helplessly away? Parents seem oblivious to this double standard. No way would even the most obtuse person think of carrying on a conversation with their

boss, sweetheart or anyone else in the morning before brushing their teeth, or after a meal which includes garlic or onions. Babies are people too, with sensibilities of what is and isn't pleasant.
**Suggestion:** Show your child the same consideration you would afford anyone else. Brush your teeth in the morning before getting in their face.

3.) This one actually makes me loose circulation in my feet when I watch it happen. It's the I've-got-a-million-things-on-my-mind-and-now-I-gotta-tie-my-kids'-shoe scenario. In this unfortunate scene either the child comes to ask for his shoe to be tied or the parent notices the shoe is untied, and with mind elsewhere ties the shoe up like a tourniquet almost in defiance that the shoe came untied, or to make sure it never comes untied again, I don't know which. But the poor kid can hardly walk once the shoe is tied and limps along on numb feet probably wishing his shoe was untied again.
**Suggestion:** There really is a foot inside that shoe. Take time to make sure the shoe is not too tight. Double tie the shoe at a comfortable looseness.

4.) My biggest pet peeve regarding children and adults is the control adults have over children's bathroom habits. I've watched children who were in misery trying to make it through church, Sunday school, classes at school, or a parents' shopping trip, having to go to the bathroom so badly they could hardly keep it together. I've watched as some of them didn't make it, and were humiliated by an accident that could have been prevented. No one seemed to notice the distressed expression on their faces or the twisting, turning, and fidgeting caused by great physical and mental discomfort. No one knows how badly or how often anyone has to use the restroom better than the person who has to go. No adult would stand around and wet their pants because another adult would not give them permission to go. But children's rights are completely at the mercy of the sensitivity (or lack thereof) of the adults who have control over them. Again, there is a tremendous double standard. Adults would never allow anyone to control them to the point of humiliation on so personal an issue. Why subject a child to these indignities?

**Suggestion:** Parents, teachers, Sunday school teachers, Den mothers or whatever, when someone tells you they need to use the restroom; don't be a control freak. You don't have their bladder or bowels, give them the benefit of the doubt and let them go. If you're a teacher and fear an avalanche of bathroom requests, have more frequent bathroom breaks. Five minutes or ten out of your schedule isn't going to stop the earths' rotation, and you might find your students better able to pay attention and participate.

5.) There are a million and one reasons for not dropping in on friends and family unannounced; they've just had a serious fight and are not in the mood to see anyone; they just sat down to dinner and there isn't enough for company; they are trying to have hard-to-come-by quality time with immediate family members, and you are interrupting; they're on a time line for getting things done and your untimely visit just blew it for them; busy couples find a minute for some personal time and your unannounced visit ruins everything. Well, you get the point. Call before you just drop in.

6.) We are not alone in the world. Be respectful of others. Don't carry on a conversation from your car with someone while a line of cars is behind you. Don't let your children's antics dominate a public scene such as a restaurant, church, or a department store and spoil the outing for others. Greeting a couple in a restaurant is perfectly fine, but don't sit down at their table for a prolonged visit. They might be out alone with intent. Take baths and wear clean clothes. Music is personal. Don't make everyone hear yours while you bump down the street to rap music at 2am or any other time of day for that matter.

7.) One can't help but notice the snarly mess that so many relationships between men and women have become. I don't claim to have all the answers and certainly the fine nuances of any relationship are tricky at times, but it seems to me that the root of most problems could be easily remedied. Relationships remind me of restaurants believe it or not. Every time a new restaurant opens the food is great, the wait staff is on the ball, and the atmosphere is designed to make you feel right at home. Visit the same restaurant a year or two later and there's less food on the plate, the quality is down and the price is up. Sometimes the wait staff is on the ball and sometimes you can't even find them. Relationships and restaurants seem to have something in common and also seem to need the same remedy. Whatever you started with, you will have to continue with at least that much in order to succeed. Women who spent two hours getting ready before a date to make sure they were sexy, sweet smelling and had every hair in place decide they don't need to bother with that so much anymore. Men who pulled out the stops to win a woman's heart feel they don't need to try anymore after they win her. Men often seem to me to be like hunters...interest at a fever pitch using every lure and ploy to score and then after the girl's in love with them, she is relegated to the trophy room in their hearts. They get all excited over a ball game and hardly give their sweetheart a glance anymore. Getting excited over sports is ok but when there's never any excitement for the one you love, your excitement has been misplaced. Taking each other for granted and then becoming dissatisfied and wondering where the fire went is a little crazy! *Nothing* works without effort!! A relationship is also a life investment. If we kept our weight down and exercised before marriage in order to be more attractive, we ought to continue to care that much after. If we were sweet, agreeable, and loving before marriage, we ought to continue to be so after. We live in a throwaway society. If something or someone doesn't please us, we throw them out and move on. There's only so much moving on you can do before you come to the end of the line and realize you're all alone. If you have a relationship, work on the problems and the relationship will be stronger and sweeter for having stuck it out. Just sayin'...

8.) If there's any one over used expression I particularly hate, it's the callous, unthinking council "Get over it." There are many things in this life from which we move on from simply because time passes but that doesn't necessarily mean that the heart has healed. Sometimes even when it does heal, if your life and responses are not the same as they were, many obtuse people will still keep chiding "Get over it." I wonder if they ever once really think about the stupid, unfeeling remark they've just made? Someone may lose a leg in an accident and for a time be so mentally bogged down that they're not able to see ahead past the tragedy, but when they finally get enough control of their mind to decide to live and move on, they still go on without the leg. Life will never be the same. They will walk differently and accommodate for the lost limb in many ways unknown to the rest of us. The same is true for those who have suffered an emotional trauma. They may go on but they will have lost something or their coping mechanisms may be quite different than someone else's. There may at times be relapses. So, I believe if you can't offer encouragement and compassion to someone not walking or feeling at the pace you've allotted as satisfactory, the best thing to do is button it up.

9.) I'd say the majority of people have a tendency to avoid anything viewed as different or strange. This is certainly a valid response when there are hitchhikers involved or some other dangerous situation, but some of the most remarkable, pleasurable, informative, lasting, strengthening, fulfilling, enlightening, loving experiences in my life, (and in the lives of those around me on whom I've been spying) were events, decisions, or people who fell into the apprehensive category of different.

The bottom line is that some of the things that might seem very different from what we are accustomed to might also be just what is needed and the best thing that's happened to us yet. Don't make snap judgments against every different thing or person. Have a closer look and make an educated judgment instead of a superstitious one based on the hearsay of others.

Concerning those who have been used to spending a lot of time alone; in beginning a relationship of any kind, it might be good to remember we don't have the same social yardstick as those who are a part of the main stream. Many of life's responses, expectations, and behaviors are formed by whatever pack we run in. We tend to think similar to those with whom we associate. But for those who don't have the privilege of association the yardstick may be altogether different. I think this is exactly how the label *geek* or any other label gets applied. In the privacy of one's own mind certain unusual or subtle things may be justly appreciated, but to the pack these same sensibilities seem superfluous or just plain strange; I mean, who thinks of that stuff anyway? But what happens in solitude is that there's so much time for introspection and examining at leisure any and every facet of life large or small that it appears as thinking too much, being too opinionated, or too serious. To those lucky souls outside of solitude who are so much a part of what is going on around them and have so much companionship, that degree of introspection may just not be as much an integral part of their lives. I'm pretty sure that most who occupy solitude would gladly trade in some of the thinking time for actual participation with others, but it doesn't always turn out that way. The question is, who would any of us be if we lived utterly alone and our world was completely uncensored? I guarantee you; you'd be doing a lot of thinking. It's a staple of solitude, welcomed or not.

A few of the past times in solitude when not taking care of business like the rest of the world could appear pretty childish if anyone happened to be observing. Since I was very young, I enjoyed dancing, and not just drawing, but coloring pictures. You who are not loners would probably think twice about telling your friends that you liked to *color*. In the so called normal world, coloring is thought to be for children and so even though an adult might enjoy it, they'd probably feel silly actually doing it and if they did, they'd never tell anyone about it! People in solitude don't have to feel silly if they like to color...after all, who cares if they do or not. There are so many things that just aren't cool after a certain point in life, and even though some people may still secretly enjoy or want to do them, they'd be embarrassed for anyone to know because the pack would frown and their coolness would be in question. An enormous blessing in solitude is a reprieve from the burden of being cool. You can skip if you feel like it or pick wild flowers, do some solo Christmas Caroling, or play outside in the rain...nobody cares.

I can recall several occasions when I heard people say that they thought it strange or even wrong when they saw someone out alone (particularly a woman) say at the movies, a restaurant, or any other place where it is more common to see couples or groups of people. In their minds the loner was strange because he or she was out alone. What an irony!! But think about it, if you were someone in solitude wouldn't you still like to eat out occasionally, see a movie, go to a concert or whatever? Should you bypass these common, pleasant experiences just because there might not be anyone to share it with? I never did. I decided long ago that I would go out and enjoy my life such as it was. Of course, it's more fun to go to the movies with someone else, laugh or cry and talk over what you saw and how you felt about it with someone else, but if that's not what your situation is, it's still better to go alone and experience what you can than not to go at all. It was a part of my decision to not let life's experiences be stolen from me simply because I didn't usually have anyone to share those experiences with.

It's not much different than someone who's physically handicapped. They can decide to be non-participants in life because they don't fit the non-handicapped standard which might be to some extent a perception that the experiences of the handicapped are incomplete and therefore invalid because after all those people can't walk or see; or the handicapped can decide to do all that is possible for them to do and fully enjoy the life they were given.

It's my sincerest belief that God has provided opportunities of happiness for each of us. It's just that so many of us have notions set in stone as to how that happiness should be realized and we're certain that the familiar is the only way it can come. Often we probably miss it simply because it's coming from an unrecognized source. I'm certain there've been a lot of missed opportunities for joy because it came in a plain brown box rather than wrapped in our ideas of it.

Of course, there's no way for me to remember everything I've seen from the walls of solitude. I probably should have been taking notes from the beginning, which I surely would have done if I'd had any idea I would someday write a book.

# Chapter 6
# Occupying Solitude

# The Fruits

So, what exactly goes on in this solitude that makes it easier to inhabit? What exactly are the fruits of my solitude for which this book is named?

I think we'd all agree that it would be ridiculous if the earth, like some people, made the proud assertion that it doesn't need anybody or anything. We know that without the sun and its precise relationship to earth, life as we know it would quickly end. Without the sun, we would just be another cold (or hot) rock in the universe. With the sun, the planet is alive and abundant with life and therefore both special and necessary.

People are no different although many have adopted a cynical attitude to mask both disappointment and need. We need the warmth, and nurture of a sun/ relationship in our lives in order to be special and alive. Without it we wither and mutate into people we were never meant to be; without it we end up in solitude where we may tell ourselves any number of things true or untrue in order to survive, but what we tell ourselves will never be enough to fill us. Some of us tell ourselves we don't need anyone, we don't need love, or maybe worst of all that there's no such thing as love.

If solitude is unrelieved over a long period of time by any real connection it becomes so painful that sometimes we feel we must tell ourselves these negative platitudes over and over again to quench the insistence of hope. It's extremely damaging emotionally to have hope crushed repeatedly, and installing the "I don't needs" is our way to protect our hearts from expectancy. There is a verse in the Bible in Proverbs that reads "Hope deferred maketh the heart sick" and it can definitely make you sick in spirit to be disappointed of a deep need repeatedly.

Common to those with too much time on their hands is run-a-way thinking. There is simply too much time to think about everything. I didn't really suffer too much from this until I was over ten years old. On occasion my loneliness would produce lethargy so hard to shake that it kept me from doing things to divert myself. There I wallowed in the reality of being alone.

At these times I became prey to some very uncomfortable frames of mind; if there was anything amiss in my body, say a bump on my arm or some other trivial thing, my thought processes would take me on an odyssey of downward spiraling illness to the place where the next thing I knew I was attending my own funeral. And then too, there were the unremitting thoughts about the reasons for my solitude, my parents troublesome relationship, my fears that it would always be this way, that I would die young, or that people I cared about would die, or my dog would die etc, etc, etc. At such times it would feel as if I were descending so far into myself that I would never see the light of day again; like falling into a well. Without a rescuer, it becomes necessary to rescue yourself as best you can. A bout of run-a-way thinking always renewed in me a fresh incentive for activity of some kind. Anything was preferable to being raked over the coals by your own mind.

The worse thing about the full time job of coping with solitude is that paradoxically, it is the salient feature of its empty self. I was alone, and all I thought of was how alone I was. It only made sense that if I wanted to survive in that wilderness, the focus of that solitude would have to undergo major reconstruction, and so I began to think of what I'd like to do if I had the chance; I began to look around me for interests to cultivate.

First and foremost, I wanted intelligent friends whom I could connect with and learn from. Also, I was keenly alive to beauty of any kind whether it was nature, music, or any of the millions of other arts; these loves could be used to furnish my island. On the one hand, whenever encountered and perused, these things made me feel alive; opposite that, my unadorned solitude, full of the pain of rejection, the constant *waiting* for something that never shows up. Without change boredom, emptiness, bitterness and the indignation of being completely unnecessary and unsolicited would be the prevailing winds of my small world.

What regrettable harvest could possibly come from allowing so many ugly and barren feelings to proliferate inside my being? I'm completely convinced that the ugliest crimes of our world could be traced back to minds and hearts that were predominantly fostered in the poisonous atmosphere of an uncultivated solitude. Besides, I wanted to experience many things and the uncultivated solitude was much too confining. Somehow it had to be stretched into satisfactory and panoramic dimensions. I had a fertile mind and spirit and varied interests. I just needed to *grow* some useful crops there.

And last, but certainly not least, I did not want to allow those who shut me out the satisfaction of watching me helplessly sit and die in the place they had seen fit to leave me in. I knew early on that I could never make it perfect; never provide for myself that sun I so needed, but I knew I could make it much better, even pleasant.

There's one particular negative tendency that steadily developed in that quiet place that's been hard for me to overcome; that of hiding. I suppose hiding is the natural reflex of many outsiders but not hiding seemed to heighten my vulnerability so, I much preferred keeping to the shadows in social settings, still, some discernment needs to be developed as to when to hide and when to come out.

Vulnerability is highly misunderstood. It's not supposed to be a bad thing though unfortunately, some people choose to abuse the vulnerabilities of those whose trust they have won to exploit it to serve their own unwholesome motives. When we think of vulnerability as something to avoid at all costs, it's really this version of it that we object to. But I believe that God designed it as an admission of and a submission to our trust in another. Being able to be vulnerable in the faith that we are loved as we love is the highest freedom we can know and certainly it is the place where we can become most real because the need to protect ourselves is no longer necessary…it's what is supposed to be going on between us and Him I believe.

Hiding was for me the by-product of the abuse of vulnerability. Because I'd had far too much experience with those who knew exactly how and where to hurt me and targeted those tender areas intentionally to draw blood, I learned to hide early on and have had a hard time coming into the open right up until this present time. It's not that I've wanted to be deceptive, it's just been my misfortune that whenever I would reveal myself in anyway, I was almost immediately punished for my trust.

Unfortunately, the way I ended up making my living collided head on with my solitude. For most of my life up to this present day my livelihood has been as a professional vocalist, which is a tricky occupation in which to hide. My local popularity has been enough that I could hardly ever go anywhere without someone recognizing me from my work and coming over to talk to me. My means of camouflage had to be carefully devised. It's probably my best art form if only anybody knew. I hide in plain sight more often than not and no one in the world would suppose that I am shy because I seem to be a very outgoing person, but it's totally possible to hide behind an elaborate wall of words and laughter. For my public performances in this area I should have had an Oscar many times over.

In the early days of my solitude before I could read, I tapped into my love of nature to comfort myself. I'm almost certain I damaged my eyesight by looking at the sun and sky which I thought the most beautiful things in the world. Since I was only four when I started to run away periodically with the family dog Dandy, a Boston terrier, and since no one knew of my solitude or of my interests, it never occurred to my folks to tell me it wasn't good to look directly at the sun. So I watched the sky intently and often spoke aloud to it as though it were a person. No matter how sad or angry or hurt I was, I always felt comforted by telling the sky which I had personified into a loving parent/guardian who cared deeply for me. I believed in my childish mind that the sky loved me and was always pleased with me, and that when I was sad it had compassion on me. Crazy as that may sound, it was a palpable guardian and not once even as an adult have I been disappointed of it or lost that perception. The sky still has a profound effect on negative moods for me, which is probably the reason I stay outdoors as much as possible.

One really advantageous fruit of solitude is the gift of time with one's self; if not resisted you can come to really know yourself in such a way that your entire life has more chance of success in that you know better how to make decisions for yourself in every aspect of your life from business decisions to a life partner. I've noticed this doesn't override the prerogative to make a bad decision by ignoring things in plain sight or canceling reason, but it generally will furnish you with enough awareness to make a sound decision if wisdom is ruling.

I haven't always been wise, but rarely was it because I didn't have adequate council; it was because I let my heart rule instead of my head. Some decisions should be made under the hearts rule; but in some areas allowing your heart to rule will destroy you.

One particular decision I made for myself that completely frustrated my family and close acquaintances was actually one of the wisest decisions I ever made for myself especially considering what was going on in my life at the time. I was twenty-one and freshly the widow of a murdered husband. Though we'd been estranged by his frequent bouts with heroin, the law, and rehab time (the last which had been a nine month program in Lexington, Kentucky from which he'd had the most success) the loss and changes I went through were extremely painful. Though he had beaten me and been inhumanly cruel not only to me but to anything he deemed helpless, I had finally come to forgive and to feel very sorry for him. Maybe it sounds crazy, and I'm not advocating that women (or men) remain in an abusive relationship, if you're in one, get out…now, but I am saying your first reflex which is to hate someone who has hurt you will ultimately destroy you; you cannot allow such corrosive feelings to expand in you. You can come to understand which allows you to have compassion on your enemy even though you mustn't cohabitate with them. I came to understand that it was not me that Phillip was hitting; it was just that I was the only one near enough to translate his pain to. He tormented the weak, because he felt weak and tormented. His premature death was a real tragedy to me.

I saw clearly how anyone might stray down any number of destructive paths when deeply hurt at not receiving their basic needs at the hands of people who are supposed to love them. I knew it firsthand. Phillips death frightened me because I was a helpless witness to and hostage of his pain and how it robbed him piece by piece of even the potential to hope for happiness which ultimately cost him his life. He was a journeyman electrician; the youngest in Michigan, he was unbelievably physically perfect, and one the most damaged people I've ever known…and dead at twenty-four.

My opportunity for big time fame came on the heels of Phillip's death. I was emotionally raw and completely bewildered. My lifelong distress at not belonging and of no real connection was not only unrelieved but greatly aggravated by the events of the past four years of my life. I couldn't make sense of the tragedy I'd been a part of nor had I any ideas of how to proceed. I felt an overwhelming desire to run away and hide for a very long time.

I don't think people in their infatuation with and unrealistic views of fame and wealth understand the price that comes with it. When we think of rock stars, movie stars, and other people who are famous, all we see is the respect, money and falsely perceived freedom we think they possess. But I think it not at all strange that so many of them fall prey to drug and alcohol abuse. No one is wonderful 24/7, but in showbiz they are expected to be and drugs and alcohol are often used to manufacture emotions they don't always feel. Being continually expected to live up to the fantasies of others is no easy thing to pull off.

I thought about being thrown into the highly volatile arena of entertainment with my ragged sense of self-worth and my neediness as almost suicidal. Standing onstage receiving the praise and adulation of hundreds or even thousands of strangers and then going back to my hotel room alone to grapple with the irony of having no real contemporary connection seemed an inevitable recipe for disaster.

Just because a person can sing or act doesn't necessarily mean the lifestyle they will most likely be living will be a healthy one for their particular emotional state as we see evidence of in Hollywood news continually; entertainers leading extremely problematic lives due to the particular stresses and expectations of the industry losing their lives in the high wire act that fame is. No wonder there is so much personal failure in their lives! Relationships require quality time and effort as do the careers of the famous. Imagine being away from your spouse and children for many months out of the year, continually in the presence of gifted, attractive people also away from their families. Imagine how the loneliness of the road and the always present temptations year after year could break down a relationship. Relationships are put on the back burner while the famous keep up their very demanding career obligations and too often fall apart due to the neglect that distance and limited time impose. But our hearts are not fed by careers…we are fed through meaningful relationships. We simply cannot have it all. Choices have to be made.

Because to me love and belonging have always been the most valuable and desired commodities, I chose not to get on the fast track of pursuing a life of fame while my emotional issues as of yet hadn't been answered. I also had a four year old son whom I was unwilling to leave for months at a time. And last, but by no means least, I was painfully aware that because of my youth and the horrendous happenings in it, I had no real sense of myself. That is a huge no-no for any major decision, but can be especially lethal in showbiz. When the news is full of entertainers who are in constant crisis regardless of their unquestionable genius and talents, the first thing that comes into speculation is the lifestyle of too much power, too much money, too much access to contraband, too much partying, and too little sense of self, and very little if any self-restraint.

Even though I missed a couple of incredible opportunities, and though many people shook their heads at my choice and just couldn't understand why I would waste such opportunities, I've never regretted my decision. I continued to play music in the Midwest which is by no means the big time, but it was quite adequate in allowing me to make a very decent living doing what I loved and did best and I was still able to be at home almost every day. Without the advantages of my solitude I don't know if I would've recognized how emotionally dangerous it would have been for me to have embarked on so demanding a career at such a crucial time in my life. Because I knew myself I understood better than anyone what it would cost me, and I knew all too well that I couldn't afford to pay it.

In this important decision the fruit of the solitude was the ability to discern what was best for me; the superficial gratification of being admired and wealthy for the personal sacrifice of emotional stability. Lest there be some gross misunderstanding about my sanity, let me say here and now that like anyone else wealth and popularity were highly attractive and to be desired, just not at the price I would then have had to pay. I feel that if those same opportunities presented themselves now, I would be ready and able to take them.

The fruits of my solitude like any other garden started out quite simply and took on dimension as time went by. The older I got, obviously the more things I could incorporate into my sequestered world. When I was very young, preschool through second grade, the things that kept me stable were my continual wanderings out of doors, and the transporting of myself into pictures that I found alluring. The older I got, the more intricate my construction of that world became. Through my school years singing, violin, dancing, horseback riding, art, acting in small summer theatre groups and writing were things I kept myself busy with.

In my adult years the raising of my children greatly enriched that solitude. I know…being with children is not exactly solitude. But when you consider that the bulk of my real human connection and conversation was with children, it still leaves the adult somewhat beached for a partnership of equality.

As they got older, they filled my world more and more and whatever was left unfulfilled, I continued to augment by every means available to me, both to satisfy a missing element in myself and also to acquaint my children with many wonders. I home schooled them, so besides their regular curriculum, there were many projects such as classes in First Aid and CPR at the Red Cross, art classes at the Art Institute, the celebrating of many holidays of different ethnicity, Chanukah being our favorite which we continued to celebrate throughout the years. A Synagogue near our home generously instructed us on how to observe the holiday, from every recipe and prayer, to the games, gifts and lighting of the candles. I'm sure many visitors who came to our home at that time of year thought us very odd. At one end of the house was our Christmas tree, and on the dining room table the Menorah.

I continued to pursue my own personal inclinations which occasionally drew the children's interest; calligraphy, oil painting and drawing, sculpting, the raising of butterflies, intricate beaded jewelry, gardening, the study of herbs, collecting herbs and processing them for medicinal uses such as salves and tinctures, studying medical text books, reading, raising rabbits, hiking, photography, and always writing. During this time I was still singing, composing music and recording, and of course, my lifelong favorite pastimes were reading, rambling, watching the sky and communing with God which richly enhanced every part of my life. Though I was far from an expert in all of these endeavors, I did extremely well in the arts particularly singing, writing and photography, and the use of herbs, and tolerably well in the rest which brought me much satisfaction.

These occupations succeeded admirably in making my solitude as comfortable as being alone can possibly be. My world was filled with the wonder of beauty, and kept me hopeful and alive to possibilities which I still believe in and await.

If I have any advice to offer anyone who is hurt and tired of being on the outside looking in at what they wish to be a part of but are currently excluded from, it's this; build your world! Don't sit idle focusing only on your exile. Be busy learning and making yourself an interesting person to know!

# Chapter 7
# Fruit for Thought

Golden slumber, heavenly splendor
seeds of fantasy shrouded scenes,
multi-colored, sleepy visions
blossom into dreams.
Return me to where I cannot reach
when consciousness masters me,
a place too deep to journey
by the light of wakefulness.

\*~\*~\*~\*~\*~\*~\*~\*~\*~\*~\*~\*~\*~\*~\*~\*~\*~\*~\*~\*~\*~\*

Sealed tightly inside my dreams…
Still comes reality
Leaking in at the seams.

\*~\*~\*~\*~\*~\*~\*~\*~\*~\*~\*~\*~\*~\*~\*~\*~\*~\*~\*~\*~\*~\*

Reflections of streetlights
glimmer in the bronze rain filled cups
of the fallen autumn leaves.
Their edges contract with the season
like brown curling scrolls
proclaiming summers' end.

\*~\*~\*~\*~\*~\*~\*~\*~\*~\*~\*~\*~\*~\*~\*~\*~\*~\*~\*~\*~\*~\*

# Snow

The air is full of merry snowflakes

spiraling in silent dances;

whispering to earth

the secret of their origin.


Their cool, sacred whiteness

a crystalline benediction;

a gentle deliberate baptism

as they melt upon my face.


*~*~*~*~*~*~*~*~*~*~*~*~*~*~*~*~*~*~*~*~*~*

## SPIDER

What has inspired such exaggerated fear,
that we should shiver when we see him?
I am overcome with childish anxiety
at his presence upon the ceiling above my bed.
Just before I go to sleep, the backslidden Hindu in me
smashes him with my shoe.
Then my formerly silent conscience plays nemesis
to the abject spider-corpse distributed between shoe and wall.
Did I think he would murder me in my sleep?
Or did I suppose there was enough silk
in his tiny spinnerets to enshroud me as I slept?
Somewhere in me is the spirit of a fly grown large.
If I kill him now, he won't get me later.
Poor spider.
We humans tend to view with apprehension anything
that has more eyes and legs than we do.
Still, we have the same Creator.

*~*~*~*~*~*~*~*~*~*~*~*~*~*~*~*~*~*~*~*~*~*

# Graveyard

Here under trees whose lowest boughs
overshadow me like the beams of a great house,
I wander among the dead.
There is a sense of reverent splendor
standing under monumental trees whose secret wisdom
has overseen the seasons
of our collective existence.
Here the generations unite.
Engraved in stone the dates of their comings and goings,
and the poignant interval between, a ringing silence.
What was their story?
Only here at last, time has extinguished all voices,
and every case is laid to rest
awaiting the verdict for each chosen path.
In the soft rise and fall of the wind,
what a strange, portentous tranquility abides
here in the anteroom to Eternity.

*~*~*~*~*~*~*~*~*~*~*~*~*~*~*~*~*~*~*~*~*~*~*~*~*

## Cycle

I pass the torch which flares as I diminish
And so proceeds the finite world
Until the words "It's finished."
But while I burn, I burn sincere
That some will know that I was here
And left some gem of worth behind
For some faint soul in time to find;
And with that feeble temporal power
Burn fervent 'til the final hour.
On we go through time and space
Continuing the human race,
Until the world one day is through
And we all stand in front of
**YOU**

*~*~*~*~*~*~*~*~*~*~*~*~*~*~*~*~*~*~*~*~*~*~*~*

## Doors

Doors closed, lock me out; doors open, let me in.
But doors half opened confuse me; lose me
In tantalizing hope which ought to die, but won't,
It seems a chance to come inside;
To know and to be known.
But a half opened door is a half opened heart,
Is an unwilling heart, is a dubious hope.
Why press through a crevice that grants no passage?
Why lean against a gate that pushes back?
A half opened door will not let me in,
But suspends like a hook the open soul
With a hope that is no hope, and a love that is no love.
And so I knock no more, but turn away and leave.
Somewhere on the serpentine road
Before the darkness meets me
Is an open door.

## Madness in the middle of my Head, In the Middle of the Night

Get your lawn chair and favorite caramel colored beverage or 'ittle Debra's snack cakes of death. We can watch the end of the world from the back yard to the songs of beached whales in A flat minor.

Do you ever wonder why so many seagulls are nowhere near the sea?--too many snacks inland. Every dumpster is a wildlife diner. I wonder if seagulls are having trouble with their cholesterol eating all those wasted Micky dee's fries.

There's a beautiful golf course nearby with a murky stream the color of brown paint running through it, and loose among the trees are the hairless squirrels and two-headed frogs; courtesy of Troo Green.

Are those stars falling or just satellites? Pass the chips and salsa. Chemical bar-b-que flavored chips are my favorite! FDA approved carcinogens really add a little kick to GMO foods, doncha think?

Is it spring or winter? I forget. I slept quite well in the thunderstorm last night, but had to shovel the walk this morning.

## Felonious "Fine!"

Sometimes I haven't fit in well simply because the eccentricities of our society rub my sensibilities the wrong way. We say we value honesty, but just try it sometime and see how out of joint everyone's nose gets when you assume they meant what they said, and respond accordingly. I'm sure that's why I've personally found my dealings with children and animals less arduous than many of my dealings with adults.

The world of grown-ups has always seemed to me to be a frightening place of constant show-downs of egos at OK Corral, or boring, unfathomable numbers (i.e. income taxes, insurance policies, mortgages, etc.), and societal games whose shifting rules you can never get right; a high-wire act from where at a moment's notice you can fall from grace into the abyss of social misfits where no one cares about you except your dog and some of your relations. And the worst part of being a grown-up is the unspoken mandate that your feelings should remain hidden unless in speaking up there is something to be gained.

There is a sizable element of people I've come up against for whom being real is only in scenarios you might find in stories like Pinocchio or the Velveteen Rabbit, but they seem to dismiss being real in everyday encounters with barely concealed condescension and disbelief, or regard it as terribly unsophisticated. Many are suspicious of anything real as though it might be another sort of game. I never did know exactly how to play the game though I suppose it's assumed that being an adult, I should know exactly what's expected and just do it.

On a bad day I still feel like gagging anytime someone asks me "How are you?" To me that question means you are seeking information; that you want to know how I am. However, in the grown-up world this question must be followed by the prescribed answer "Fine!" no matter what ordeals have been your recent plight, "Fine!" is already registering in the brains of the askers even before you have spoken. Any other answer is presumptuous of both the time and interest of the one asking how you are. I, on the other hand, feel extreme irritation that someone would ask about me in the name of social protocol and expect me to play along even if it means lying.

To relieve my own aggravation I decided the best way to handle the "How are you?" issue is if I see that someone really doesn't want to know how I am, I just answer their question with another question (usually the very question they just asked me) which they always answer never noticing that I didn't answer them or sometimes I answer the question with "That's qualified information." Usually this disrupts the robot response mode. If they become curious enough to inquire further, then I might feel emboldened to actually answer the simple question "How are you?"

There are many social bug-a-boos ranging from where someone's Ex should be seated at a family wedding, to the heated tumult about abolishing the N word (it should be deleted though I don't see that happening in the near future in my neighborhood), but "How are you?" is definitely a pet peeve of mine. So, I just thought I would take the opportunity in this book to air that grievance, in the event that maybe next time you get ready to ask that question you might pause before you do and ask yourself first if you really want to know the answer. If you don't really want to know, don't ask.

*~*~*~*~*~*~*~*~*~*~*~*~*~*~*~*~*~*~*~*~*~*~*

## Submission

Hiding hopeful eyes,
viewing earth while in disguise,
nothing seen can bring surprise
to this jaded heart of mine.

Next time when I stand down
from clouds of smoke to quaking ground,
love like an army will surround
this jaded heart of mine.

I know under that healing touch
my willing soul that bled too much
will shiver as it feels love clutch
this jaded heart of mine.

*~*~*~*~*~*~*~*~*~*~*~*~*~*~*~*~*~*~*~*~*~*~*

Deafness is not a testimony against sound.
And the sun, the sea, and the sky
are not less realin the absence of sight.
Just so, I am true
even in the abyss of your doubt.

*~*~*~*~*~*~*~*~*~*~*~*~*~*~*~*~*~*~*~*~*~*~*

Suspended…
Between hope and fear of hope,
I tread the wondering hours of the night;
like one shipwrecked,
longing to be at rest…to be safe at last.

## Fig Leaves and Other Coverings

I stand in the open, exposed, inside out and naked to the light.
        If you come out, I will remain. If you stay hidden,
                then I must vanish like mist inhaled by sunbeams.

Sometimes I feel like the only one unmasked at the masquerade.
I romp in Eden still, wearing only my troubled aura
    and wondering why in the fullness of springtime all the fig trees
        are missing their leaves.

So long have you evaded discovery,
        that now even you are hard-pressed to answer the question
            "Who am I?"

When will it be safe to come out?
Must we spend life crouching behind subterfuges?
Feasting yet empty…reveling in the puddle of our flesh
        while the sea of spirit lies unexplored?

Our skins touch in a fever to know and be known
though the real consummation has yet to take place.
Enter me with heart, and arms flung wide, and trust flaming
                              or not at all
                                    not at all
                                          not at all…

*~*~*~*~*~*~*~*~*~*~*~*~*~*~*~*~*~*~*~*~*~*~*~*

## TEARS

      I see the world through a teardrop;

Prisms of reflected pain

      Tear shaped pain…

    salty pain   distilled pain

Running down from eye…to cheek,

     to chin,

      to sleeve,

    from me…for you.

Please stop

     them

      from

       falling.

*~*~*~*~*~*~*~*~*~*~*~*~*~*~*~*~*~*~*~*~*~*

## Paradise Unsaid

Much spoken...though nothing said;
much said...but nothing revealed;
A wall of words to keep reality at bay.
Words like decoys leading away from disclosure.
Words like traps set to imprison another
within a consumptive will.
Words; a camouflage of flashing scenery,
brilliant with thespian genius
and tales of success, and of life on the mountaintops
while behind them, the speaker is dying slowly, poignantly,
with salvation merely the length of truth away.

The only thing sadder than untrue words
is the soul who can't see past them.
In fear they negate the thrust of true words
against the gates of their hearing,
Their words flow like fog from their lips
to obscure the vision of an honest heart.
Thus hidden, the horizon contracts
to the limits of their eyesight.
They lie inside their flesh as in a tomb
waiting only for the lights to go out.

*~*~*~*~*~*~*~*~*~*~*~*~*~*~*~*~*~*~*~*~*~*

## Circles

It's not that there isn't enough love to go around
That's causing all the discontent;
it's the direction of that love that causes all the heartache.
The river seems to flow away from one's self;
We love someone, who loves someone else, who loves another;
And on it goes until it comes to the one who loves us
But them we do not love.

The miracle of love, like conception, is when
It takes root in the heart we've given it to
And returns to us from that same heart.

*~*~*~*~*~*~*~*~*~*~*~*~*~*~*~*~*~*~*~*~*~*~*

## Wise and Otherwise Sayings

Some days are rebellious from beginning to end,
Contending even with ourselves
when other victims are not available.
Whenever we are at odds with ourselves for whatever reason,
it will color all else encountered in shades of battle.

*~*~*~*~*~*~*~*~*~*~*~*~*~*~*~*~*~*~*~*~*~*~*~*~*

Unexpressed love is a form of sterility.

*~*~*~*~*~*~*~*~*~*~*~*~*~*~*~*~*~*~*~*~*~*~*~*~*

Never bypass the present to get to the future.
In so doing you might arrive at your destination only to find you
are sadly lacking something you should have brought with you.

*~*~*~*~*~*~*~*~*~*~*~*~*~*~*~*~*~*~*~*~*~*~*~*~*

Anyone who withholds the sharing of a positive feeling with the
object of those feelings ought to check their motive for silence.
Too often pride is the prohibiting cause. Sometimes we feel
a little less in control when our hearts are known…but then again,
if it's control you want, try being an animal trainer.

*~*~*~*~*~*~*~*~*~*~*~*~*~*~*~*~*~*~*~*~*~*~*~*~*

Unbelief is a thief and a murderer leaving its victims bereft of
possibilities.

*~*~*~*~*~*~*~*~*~*~*~*~*~*~*~*~*~*~*~*~*~*~*~*~*

Some days seem so dark, that even hope feels like an intruder.

*~*~*~*~*~*~*~*~*~*~*~*~*~*~*~*~*~*~*~*~*~*~*~*~*

Death is always near when you dwell on it,
but when you live life to the fullest,
it recedes to its appointed time.

\*~\*~\*~\*~\*~\*~\*~\*~\*~\*~\*~\*~\*~\*~\*~\*~\*~\*~\*~\*~\*

Communication creates closeness.
The lack of it creates distance.
Communication provides understanding.
The lack of it generates confusion.
Communication opens a door.
The lack of it closes the door.
So, speak or leave.

\*~\*~\*~\*~\*~\*~\*~\*~\*~\*~\*~\*~\*~\*~\*~\*~\*~\*~\*~\*~\*

The conscience of an invalidator is clear;
needs do not have to be met
because they do not exist.

\*~\*~\*~\*~\*~\*~\*~\*~\*~\*~\*~\*~\*~\*~\*~\*~\*~\*~\*~\*~\*

# Chapter 8
# An Inspirational Solitude

# God vs. Religion

My friends and family who knew this book was in the works wondered if it would be religious reading because the main thread of the story was my search for God in the midst of my solitude. After carefully thinking it over I decided that it was not a religious book at all. It is the story of my journey in which God was the focal point, not religion.

As you can see by my accounts there was never any loyalty toward any church I attended that would not evaporate in a hurry if I did not find what I was looking for. I meant no disrespect in leaving one church for another. I simply was looking for something or more to the point, Someone I didn't find. Even after I found what I had so long searched after, I've still hesitated to call myself a Christian.

The word Christian means Christ-like. Not one time in my life no matter how many churches I went to or how much progress I made in God, did I ever feel worthy enough to announce myself a Christian to others. Even though I am much improved by my association with Jesus and my efforts to conform myself into something He could be at least a little pleased with, I am still acutely aware of how short of the mark I fall. So, I'm much more comfortable with someone else coming to the conclusion that I am a Christian than with proclaiming myself to be one.

This is not to be mistaken for any shame of my Christian walk, but it reminds me of a person who's beautiful; it's much better for someone else to think they're beautiful and to say so, than for them to go around tooting their own horn and expecting the world to make exceptions for them because of it. Also, unfortunately there have been many people touting their Christianity and involvement in their local church that were later found to be serial killers, child molesters, or connected with any number of other unsavory crimes. Obviously, they did not have the goods from God that they claimed to have, and their deeds reflected badly on religion and turned away many people and destroyed the faith of those earnestly seeking God.

These poems I hope will reflect the love and praise I have for my Sovereign Lord, Jesus Christ.

# Compassion

A beggar sought a crust of bread
Within the village square,
Perception caused his heart to dread
His eyes reflect despair.

Upon each soul his need did knock
And to his silent pleading
Each face appeared as granite rock
Deliberate and unheeding.

Covertly eyes regarded him;
Took in his voiceless woe;
Then averting, so despised him,
Believing he would never know.

Each one he ventured to approach
Pretended not to see,
Or quenched him with a cool reproach
In effort to be free.

In weariness his head was bowed
Considering his plight;
One shadow from within the crowd
Obscured remaining light.

The shadow lingered on him long,
So long, he felt it touch him.
A hand was proffered clean and strong
As though it would uplift him.

Brief espial revealed a man
Before him richly dressed;
So well he seemed to understand,
His eyes great ruth expressed.

What chill the beggar had sustained
From those who had abhorred him,
The warmth the rich man's smile contained
Exalted and restored him.

The promised help, the real concern
Were balm unto his soul.
The rich man's motive he would learn;
His history unfold.

Out from the lined and careworn face
Encouragement came flowing.
Upon his cheek a tear would trace
An inward grief now showing.

The beggar longed to speak out free;
The question in him burned,
"Why would you help a man like me
That all the world has spurned?"

The rich man seeing him confounded
Led him not to misconstrue;
The mystery fled when his voice sounded,
"I once was a beggar, too."

*~*~*~*~*~*~*~*~*~*~*~*~*~*~*~*~*~*~*~*~*~*

## Escort through Sorrow

Beneath a bowered arch was I,
Good fortune full and green;
And awed at all who with me stood
To on my blessing lean.

Companions of the sunshine
Through light and beauty do abide,
As long as I shall prosper
They will be here at my side.

But in the midst of halcyon days
Affliction may come stealing,
Replacing mirth and joyous song
For tearful prayers appealing.

Upon the far horizon
Dark clouds form the coming night;
While some inkling of the future
Puts all shallow hearts to flight.

I sought with misted vision
As the night fell hard and cold;
To find one heart to beat with mine,
One single hand to hold.

My solitude felt so complete
It seemed I scarce could stand,
When beneath my failing strength
Was passed a bleeding hand.

It held me hard and fast in love
'til daylight filtered through
Revealing all the night had held
in Heavenly revue.

I really never was alone,
Nor in my sorrow lonely;
Traveling on the shadowed path
Sustained by Jesus only.

## Thomas Newman

I first discovered Thomas Newman when I went to see the movie, The Horse Whisperer. I fell instantly in love with his music, and with each successive encounter with his music, I became more and more besotted with his spirit and unique, sensitive style.

In the first year that I knew his music it was all I listened to. Whenever I watched a movie in which he had written the score, I recognized him as soon as the first chords reached my ears. I'm always aware of music wherever I am, but especially where soundtracks are concerned, I don't generally recognize the artist. It's just great music, or not. Only Thomas Newman's soundtracks are distinguished in my hearing.

Let it be said here and now, that there are many wonderfully gifted artists who stir and inspire me greatly, it's just that if I were stranded on a desert island and allowed only one artists' music, it would be Thomas Newman hands down. Everything about his music enchants me; choice of articulation for the instruments, the way he uses woodwinds and strings, the grace, magic, and emotion in every measure.

When I need to think deeply on a matter, it's his music that opens the channels of honest thinking in me. It polishes every good thing in me; probes and uncovers long hidden places in my thoughts and feelings. I definitely think God timed Thomas Newman's introduction into my life perfectly, and yes, I do believe that he is a gift from God.

If my life were a movie, his would be the only music to describe it. Up until the time I was first introduced to his music, my memories only went back to about four years old. I know it sounds a little crazy, but after I began listening to him every day, a gate in my memory opened to reveal events that occurred up to two years prior to the last ones I could access. It was really quite exciting and totally unexpected.

His music has been present with me in my solitude since I discovered it, and has always enhanced it in a pleasurable, productive, and positive ways. Pleasurable, in that he has a way of transporting you to the richness of every positive emotion; productive, in that sometimes the music was a light shined on a sore place in the spirit, where the sooner there was recognition and acknowledgement, healing began. Positive in that I am always uplifted and aware of beauty when I hear it.

It would certainly be a dream-come-true if someday I actually met him!

# Afterword
## Who Are We?

It seems to me that the vast majority of people are not sure who they really are, and of course that can be a real problem when you're trying to make important decisions that will affect your life deeply and for a long time. How can you make plans for someone you don't know?

Our consciousness is constantly bombarded. Our world decides what we will view as humorous; what clothes are in and who is a geek; what size to be, what foods to eat, what places to go; what car is cool and on and on. Images are continually presented in a format which will produce in us the response best geared to benefit whoever desires our patronage. There is no area of our being that is not targeted for the benefit of another.

Magazines, television, churches, special interest groups, celebrities, and schools are all telling us who we are or who we should be. In such ways our character is developed (or stifled). We become resources to be harvested by those who hope to make a living off the seeds they have planted in our minds. It's not hard to select or identify with any or all of the above and never go any farther. But as they say; close, but no cigar. Keeping it real demands that we know who we are aside from labels others may have assigned us or images others try to lead us to assume to suit a private agenda.

The purpose of this book is essentially to point out the virtues of solitude. It is one of the biggest aids to finding out not only about you, but also, to glean valuable knowledge about human behavior in general. In learning some universal truths about human beings, you gain valuable insight into what is realistic and balanced. Without the panoramic view from solitude, your sense of balance sometimes becomes limited to your own experience. You may feel unjustly besieged, forgotten, or unappreciated, unless you look around and see that compared with the fate of many; you're actually not doing too badly. Besides, solitude can become a dangerous and extremely unpleasant place to be if you spend most of your alone time commiserating with yourself over the unfair nesses of life.

Even if it takes time to gain what you wish to gain, the interim will be profitably and pleasantly spent making you a more relaxed and fulfilled person. People in solitude want and deserve companionship, but the sad truth is that we are much less likely to see these needs met if we are filled with anxiety, anger, sadness, and neediness. Unfortunately, these manifestations, unfairly acquired as they may sometimes be, do not attract their just mitigation. More often than not, human nature tends to run away from rather than to the very appearance of need.

Do whatever it takes to keep hope and faith alive and above all, find out who you really are!

Have a safe and productive solitude!

The Beginning is Near!

Author, Stephenie Monear-Schindler

Made in the USA
Monee, IL
01 December 2021